I0804842

Warm Wishes from Sunny St. Pete

Warm Wishes from Sunny St. Pete

THE SUCCESS STORY *of* PROMOTING THE SUNSHINE CITY

Nevin D. Sitler

THE History PRESS

Published by The History Press
Charleston, SC 29403
www.historypress.net

All photographs taken from the archives of the St. Petersburg Museum of History and the author's personal collections unless otherwise noted.

First published 2014

Manufactured in the United States

ISBN 978.1.62619.274.4

Library of Congress CIP data applied for.

Public Relations Director John Lodwick...accounted for hundreds of columns of city publicity which otherwise would have been impossible to obtain.

—from a 1942 published eulogy

St. Petersburg was the first American city to hire a public relations director and the first to initiate a successful advertising budget.

CONTENTS

PREFACE

The success of early twentieth-century St. Petersburg as a tourist destination was due to consistent self-promotion highlighting the natural and physical features of peninsular Pinellas County.

Warmed by balmy Tampa Bay breezes, St. Petersburg had been dubbed by late nineteenth-century doctors as the "Health City." This tiny 1890s coastal town of fewer than three hundred inhabitants, now blessed with a slogan, new train tracks and railway pier, was an ideal setting for tourism. By 1902, advertising and newspaper articles declared St. Petersburg a city second to none.

Over the next half century—from the Building Boom to the Baby Boom—Florida, and certainly St. Petersburg, underwent a transformation. Ranked twenty-seventh nationally, the prewar Sunshine State was the South's least populated, but boosters such as John Lodwick, "tin-canners" and a world at war brought many changes, few of which escaped St. Petersburg.

More than almost any other Florida city, St. Petersburg relied on an endlessly repeated message in postcards, newspaper editorials, print advertisements and radio/television commercials marketing itself as the nation's playground, a southern garden of perpetual well-being.

That St. Petersburg was the first American city to hire a public relations director and the first to initiate a successful advertising budget speaks to the scope of this message.

In the late 1940s, while northern newspaper subscribers were teased with wintertime ads sending *Warm Wishes from Sunny St. Pete*, a series of city-funded

films was released. These quasi-documentaries, shown in countless lodges and auditoriums, portrayed the "Sunshine City" as the city of fun and sun. Without reserve, the films touted St. Petersburg as *the* ideal destination for the nation's soon-to-be senior citizens.

Warm Wishes from Sunny St. Pete explores a portion of Florida's tourism history and the city's goal of promoting St. Petersburg.

Kevin D. Sitler

INTRODUCTION

I'm going down to Florida.
Gonna get some sand in my shoes.
Gonna ride that Orange Blossom Special
And lose these New York blues.
—Johnny Cash, "Orange Blossom Special"

Florida.

For many, just saying the name conjures up thoughts of sand and surf or palm trees and sunshine. For others, it may be dreams of mild winters or wild abandonment.

Whatever one's fancy, Florida, at one time or another, probably promoted it. In fact, Florida's emergence from the territorial wilderness of the early nineteenth century to a tourist mecca nearly two hundred years later is the result of decades of boosterism by homesteaders, hucksters, salesmen and suckers—all competing to capture their "Florida Dream."

Locally, St. Petersburg's tourism industry was born from the nearly ritualistic manner adopted by the medical and military men of the 1800s, who, after spending time in the area, spoke and wrote of the pleasant coastal climate and natural abundance.

Many of these characters packaged and promoted the environment in fanciful penmanship, praising the vigorous settings. Others, upon retirement or completion of their enlistment, simply moved to the peninsula and let their livelihoods and newfound longevity speak for nature's therapeutic gifts. Regardless of their methods of success—and their failings—in those early days of St. Petersburg, the Pinellas Peninsula was a secret no longer. Through decades of grand schemes and larger dreams, few resisted the chance to croon over St. Petersburg's charm and allure.

Ever since the United States set its sights on obtaining Florida from the Spanish in the early 1800s, tourism remained an activity for the exceedingly wealthy. But with a gradual decrease in transportation costs coinciding with a rise in personal profits, traveling for pleasure increased. Tourism in the early years of the twentieth century was an untapped consumable, advertised extensively and created to a large degree by private-sector groups and growing tourist cultures. Simply put, tourism became a product for sale.

Spurred on by mail-order catalogues and print advertisements, as well as self-expression and social status, the burgeoning twentieth-century consumer and leisure class happily responded to the national trend of "conspicuous consumption." The elite masses that could afford such obvious displays of material wealth did so in a conscious effort to increase social position, real or imagined, and advertisements persuaded the influential by telling them what they should want.

The advent of advertising was a late nineteenth-century breakthrough for magazine publishers. With thousands of pamphlets, periodicals and church house publications spreading the gospel, producers of "patent" medicine and tonics found the perfect promotional tool in print. Tonic sales and circulations soared. That publications could, and still do, generate more revenue through selling display or copy space (featuring art, photos or text, respectively) than subscription sales highlights the influence and power of promotion to the consuming public.

Although southerners had favored travel to northern climes, the growth of tourism into southeastern coastal resorts in the Carolinas, Georgia and Florida was primarily a post–Civil War development. Following the war, growing numbers of northerners sought southern destinations when the winter season arrived, prompting author Ledyard Bill to affirm in his 1869 work, *A Winter in Florida*, that Florida visitors increased by the thousands annually.

"Florida has attracted considerable attention as a winter resort for invalids and pleasure-seekers," persists Bill, "where the invalid can find equable and mild temperature through the greater portion of the year."

By the turn of the twentieth century, as settlers came to inhabit the southern portion of Florida, railroads were king. Pioneer princes Henry M. Flagler and Henry B. Plant shrewdly built enormous lavish hotels fit for royalty along their railways. Packed with cash crops like lumber, phosphate

Railroad development was more prolific along the Atlantic Coast side of Florida, thanks to developers like Flagler and Plant. Still, rail travel brought increasing numbers of northern visitors to the isolated Pinellas Peninsula.

and citrus from the South, railcars rolled north only to return with a different kind of cash crop—wealthy northern folk searching for a winter escape. Those who could not afford the hefty rail fees often dared the journey via horse and buggy. Upon arrival, these vacationers sought respite from the blustery cold in opulent rail-side hotels. Most returned north enamored with the subtropical weather and sandy shores.

Prompted by the enticing railroad schedules and hotel handbills that lured thousands to visit Florida, the *Brooklyn Eagle*, in 1898, boldly labeled Florida's west coast "the Mecca of health seekers." As for upstart St. Petersburg, "where there is a large winter colony to enjoy the small fishing which abounds," the *Eagle* announced, "probably no strip of shore in Florida offers so great a number of pleasant little resorts as does Point Pinellas, and surely no place can exceed it in the charm of its climate."

Sunny tales and steel rails laid the foundation for tourism in early modern Florida. If the 1800s were a time of nurturing and cultivating the tourism industry in Florida, then the early 1900s were decades of reaping the first harvest, and coupled with advancements in transportation technology, the crop was abundant, indeed.

As the Progressive era under President Taft came to define peace, financial prosperity and population growth, upwards of five million automobiles competed with outdated agrarian modes of transportation. Thanks to Benz's and Daimler's achievements with the internal combustion engine and Ford's advancements in the automobile assembly process, America was speeding its way to becoming a nation on the move.

Before long, advertisers—freshly admonished by the government for peddling miracle remedies—focused on promoting necessities for the soaring numbers of automobile enthusiasts. While the reality of war engulfed the lives of Europeans, businesses like Cadillac, Kodak and cosmetics cajoled money-spenders in the United States. As the country braced for war, sellers of luxury items and military-recruiting campaigns vied against each other for precious newspaper advertising space. Products shamelessly evoked patriotism and pride through their promotions, while encouraging purchasers to participate in the war effort.

Commercial and governmental campaigns were not, however, the only promotional programs competing for a national audience. For Florida cities that recognized the significance of seasonal visitors, advertising in northern papers became the norm. As early as December 1918, city officials in tourist-dependent St. Petersburg sought a staggering sum to advertise the city during the current tourist season.

"If spending $20,000 to advertise St. Petersburg over the next 40 days brings here 5,000 people," insisted the board of trade president, "$2,250,000 will be put in circulation in the city." Charles Carter's predictions of profit were enough to inspire the local Liberty Loan Organization to agree. Fundraising began the following Monday.

The landmass encompassing St. Petersburg is a peninsula, geographically similar to the state of Florida. With the Gulf of Mexico and Boca Ciega Bay lapping on its western shores, and Tampa Bay surrounding the southern and eastern portions of the city, early travel options were limited. Strategically, a straight shot less than ten miles eastward across the bay would find you on the western shores of Tampa, yet realistically, a rowboat took more muscle than minutes while sailboats relied on unpredictable winds.

For water crossings, steamboats and ferries were the most popular choices. Landlubbers wishing to visit the "Cigar City" had few alternatives but to journey nearly fifty miles north from the city of St. Petersburg and then proceed overland to points east and south. A round-trip excursion could take days. Prior to World War I, travel by rail remained the surest route into Florida; before then, it was via boat or buggy or on foot.

America's love affair with the automobile fueled the growth for extensive highway development in the United States. By 1930, in Florida alone,

Compared to many early Florida "roads," this hard-surfaced route was considered by 1920s motorists to be a "super highway."

several thousand miles of hard surface crisscrossed the state, connecting fishing hamlets on the coasts to mainland merchants. In the 1920s, however, one geographical obstacle loomed for the small coastal town of St. Petersburg: isolation.

Situated mostly on the southern portion of the Pinellas Peninsula, halfway down Florida's west coast, the city of St. Petersburg was a specific destination point; rarely would a traveler be "just passing through." This was soon to change, dramatically.

During the dawn of the twentieth century, the shift in transportation from railroads and steamships to the automobile marked the decline of tourism as elitist, exclusive and expensive. On their own dime, and more importantly on their own time, auto travelers could now explore and inspect the state, making as many side trips as their passengers and fuel tank allowed. Those who chose to remain, according to handbooks with tempting titles such as *Florida in the Making*, could set up small farm-truck operations on the side of nearly any traveled tourist thoroughfare and sell Florida fruits and vegetables to the swelling ranks of visitors.

"Seeing any part of America is a pleasant and profitable experience," claimed a 1930 state-created solicitation; however, "seeing Florida gives the greatest possible returns for time and money spent." Publications did more than seek socialites, salesmen and sightseers; they told of history and fantasy that dripped with opportunity for many.

To fully grasp the influence of travelogues of the day, consider the following descriptive title: *A Guide to Florida: "The Land of Flowers," Containing A Historical Sketch, Geographical, Agricultural and Climatic Statistics, Routes of Travel by Land and Sea, and General Information Invaluable to the Invalid, Tourist or Emigrant.* Often financed by budding Florida industries, writers expressed absolute authority in their topics by inclusion of such subtitles.

Another example further illustrates this point: *Camping and Cruising in Florida: An Account of Two Winters Passed in Cruising Around the Coasts of Florida as Viewed from the Standpoint of an Angler, a Sportsman, a Yachtsman, a Naturalist, and a Physician.*

Credentials worked; doctors-turned-authors proclaimed Point Pinellas to be "one of the most salubrious and healthful locations on the west coast," and few anglers could pass up tales of fish so thick that "they impede the passage of boats" in the Tampa Bay waters.

The southbound sick received their share of counsel as well. "Surely—to the sensitive invalid, the over-taxed student, or the worn out weary businessman, seeking rest and recruitment—no place on earth can surpass," noted Daniel Tyler in 1881.

Switching roles from guide to general practitioner, Tyler instructed the ailing to observe eight imperatives, seven of which audaciously involved recouping in Florida. Dispensing advice to invalids and tourists throughout, Tyler's *Where to Go in Florida* concludes with advertisements for hotels and amenities along the route.

Alterations in lodging and improvements with the automobile led to an expansion in Florida's tourist industry in several ways. New destinations and tourist traps sprouted up along Florida's fledgling highway system.

Unquestionably, the automobile unlatched the gate to a perpetual paradise for many, altering tourist destinations while encouraging exploration into the unknown. The Depression years radically restricted the distance one could travel and the funding tourists were willing to put forth. Nevertheless, Florida's proximity to the populated East Coast states and overall lower cost of living likely enticed more than a quarter million visitors in 1930 alone.

Many Florida cities discarded any notion of becoming a manufacturing- or industry-based society, preferring to capitalize on the tourist industry instead. St. Petersburg, Florida, was one such community.

Chapter one, "Bridging the Gaps," demonstrates how the development and promotion of railroads, bridges and infrastructure transformed much of Florida and, more specifically, the isolated city of St. Petersburg, which grew from fewer than three hundred residents in 1900 to nearly thirty thousand in just two decades. The 1920s building boom and its subsequent bust are discussed in this section in addition to the nationwide economic depression's effect on advertising the city.

Continuing with the Great Depression, chapter two depicts the Sunshine City as "the City that Advertising Built." This portion examines the influence of civic leaders and the chamber of commerce, as well as the "sunshine offer" and advertisements that blanketed the nation. The discussion involves the city's goal since its incorporation as one that promotes luxury and the good life on Florida's Gulf Coast. Several featured media formats, such as postcards, newspapers, hotel handbills and letters to northern editors, relentlessly reiterate this quest.

Displays at trade shows, civic clubs and even retail storefronts were a popular method of promotion for St. Petersburg by the mid-1950s.

Hundreds of army air corps trainees fill the Sunshine City baseball field to do what military trainees do best: hurry up and wait.

A historical account of St. Petersburg and its dedication to tourism would be far from complete without extensive recognition of John Harris Lodwick, St. Petersburg's first publicity director. Lodwick's clever antics and inimitable style, along with samples of his promotional prowess and "techniques," illustrate his impact on this growing Florida city.

From the installation of St. Petersburg's celebrated green benches to housing Goodyear blimps, civic leaders and promoters vied for national attention—and it worked. Census figures indicate that a doubling occurred from one decade to the next. This rapid growth was due to several factors: the automobile, postwar prosperity and transportation improvements. Moving on to chapter three, we deal with "War and Beyond" and some of the opinion molders who followed in John Lodwick's footsteps.

As war loomed ever closer, massive military camps and obscure bases filled Florida's landscape with more than 2 million military trainees. St. Petersburg alone received in excess of 100,000 airmen, seaman and soldiers.

On the homefront, the promotional efforts during the war years enticed some to continue their patriotic duty of keeping fit for "the war effort," and there was no better place than St. Petersburg to get your vitamins A, D and V—for victory.

Throughout the global conflict, brazen advertisements evoked patriotism and reminded readers of Florida's potential. At the conclusion of World War II, there was a massive migration of soldiers and their sweethearts, now financially backed by GI Bill home loan guarantees. Added into that mix were Florida's booming retiree population, construction of Bay Pines—the largest VA hospital in the South—and a renewed attitude of postwar prosperity. The result was a rapid modernization of this once-sleepy fishing hamlet and a redoubled emphasis on selling St. Petersburg.

Chapter One

BRIDGING THE GAPS

"A pretty good place for a settlement," English cartographer George Gauld noted on several manuscript charts of Tampa Bay in the eighteenth century. Gauld's prophecy, written in the summer of 1765 while charting the navigability of Florida's west coast, covered the southern tip of present-day Pinellas County. Florida, having come into the hands of the British two years prior, served as a distraction for many colonists. By using the newly acquired lands of East and West Florida, Great Britain hoped to keep at bay those wanderlust souls who felt restricted by the Proclamation of 1763. Even though this proclamation outlawed travel west over the Appalachians, there was plenty of land to be had in the new fourteenth and fifteenth British "colonies" of Florida.

Trading the captured port capital of Havana for Florida in 1763, Great Britain ruled over its new holdings for a mere twenty years. The British government, following two decades of lackluster attempts to populate the remote locale, "concluded suddenly that it was worthless to retain the province of Florida."

With the removal of British inhabitants, Sidney Lanier penned in 1875 that Florida returned to the wilds from which it was born. "A Spanish lethargy settled upon the land," Lanier claimed. He further noted that Florida, "torn with Indian fights, and with irregular conflicts of adventuring parties and of ill-advised republican frontiersmen," came into the nineteenth century with much bloodshed.

In place of the dispossessed and destroyed native tribes of Spanish Florida, fleeing bands of Georgia and Carolina Creeks moved into the area. Saddled with what is probably the Spanish term for "runaway" or "wild one," Florida's new Indian inhabitants, the Seminoles, were simply no match for the relentless efforts of the U.S. government to maintain possession and control of Florida.

Expensive and unpopular throughout the nation, the Indian Wars garnered an antiwar consensus. The decades-long conflict was too costly to continue hunting for a few desperado tribes hidden in Florida scrub and swampland. The United States, after decades of warfare and millions of dollars, decided to unilaterally remove troops and allow the small number of natives to remain. However, by the war's end in 1858, the Seminoles had been methodically eliminated, or migrated, through years of want, warfare and disease. In the Tampa Bay region, Florida's natives had all but vanished. In their place came the investors, curious souls and infirm who eventually secured the Pinellas Peninsula's mighty role in the tourist industry.

Flagler and Plant

The Builders

Several events stimulated the tourist trade in Florida during the closing of the nineteenth century. First, southern boosters viewed tourism as a crucial element in post-Reconstruction recovery as a way to jumpstart a depressed economy. The second and possibly greatest impact came throughout the final decades of the nineteenth century as luxury hotels, both inland and on the coastal edges, sprouted up from the loamy soils of the Sunshine State. In St. Augustine, Henry Flagler of Standard Oil fame constructed the Ponce de Leon and the Alcazar Hotels, while obtaining a third, which he christened the Cordova. Revitalizing the old fort city, he also built needed churches and hospitals while connecting the city with power, water and sewer services.

Recognizing the lack of suitable transportation into St. Augustine—and to his investments—Henry Flagler bought and rebuilt a short-line railroad company to make his hotels more accessible. By 1885, now in the hotel and railroad business, Flagler connected and improved additional railroad lines northward to Jacksonville and, more importantly, southward down the east coast of Florida. From Ormond Beach and then to Palm Beach in 1893, Flagler supported his system of rails and hotels through extensive improvements along each destination, constructing waterworks, utilities, city halls and courthouses.

Flagler, however, was not alone. His "keen-minded Connecticut Yankee" counterpart, Henry B. Plant, had his sights set on Florida's west coast. Though operating on opposite coasts, both Plant and Flagler recognized "Americans' love affair with the beach," noted Florida historian Gary Mormino in *Land of Sunshine State of Dreams*, and they constructed "ornate hotels along the Atlantic and Gulf coasts, that defied seaside architecture."

A 1938 Florida travel book by Frank Stockbridge and John Perry went as far as stating that "nothing more spacious in the way of a hotel probably has ever been built anywhere in the world at any time."

Constructed to rival anything in Flagler's arsenal of amenities, the Tampa Bay Hotel featured over five hundred rooms and a grand hall that accommodated 1,500 merrymakers. The elegance and extravagance of the hotel's idyllic settings prompted visitors to describe "the greatest hotel in the world" as a grand structure in which guests could relax and marvel at the luxurious grounds.

While hundreds of laborers and artisans began construction on the Tampa Bay Hotel in 1888, a Russian railroad mogul named Peter Demens ran his raggedy rail line across the bay into a sparsely populated village—St. Petersburg.

Flagler and Plant shaped an alluring image of Florida. Their efforts and friendly rivalry tempted tourist and sanitarium seekers to visit the state, while encouraging businesses and other men of means, like Demens, to buy into the Florida fantasy, repackage it and sell it to others at a profit. The development of tourism in Florida strengthened exponentially as the nineteenth century ended. While tourists' fondness for Florida rose with each passing year, their mode of arrival evolved even faster.

Peter Demens.

Driving the Growth

Henry Ford's 1908 introduction of the Model T sparked a new American Revolution. His affordable, mass-produced automobile offered the mobility and freedom that neither trains nor horse and buggy could. The middle classes could now afford to purchase automobiles. Florida's roads and freeways were rapidly tested.

In response, resort communities like St. Petersburg experienced a yearly invasion of "average citizens" descending on the town in horseless carriages. Traversing hundreds of weather-beaten miles and intending to stave off the cold of the North with balmy winds from the Gulf of Mexico and Tampa Bay, these tourists often became seasonal and permanent inhabitants.

The temporary wartime economic lull in tourism brought on by the First World War gave way to the early 1920s boom felt in many Florida cities. The postwar influx of permanent residents in St. Petersburg—retirees and returning doughboys coupled with wishful schemers and the seasonal tin can tourists—led to intense land acquisitions and real estate dealings. What started out as fields of tents, shanties and lean-tos packed with money-conscious visitors soon grew into residential housing and storefronts.

Promoting the Pinellas Peninsula was a full-time job for many. Some disciples of the promotional movement acted out of true love for the area; others promoted St. Petersburg for possibly the more practical reason of building personal wealth. The efforts and escapades of these promoters weren't necessarily get-rich-quick schemes, but they weren't altogether altruistic either.

William "Alligator Man" Carpenter is a case in point. Bill was the proprietor of the city's first theater, the Royal Palm, an attraction for both locals and tourists because it not only showed movies but also raised, displayed and sold alligators at the venue. Some folks were alarmed at William's claim of maintaining an inventory of as many as one thousand of the prehistoric critters penned up behind his cinema. But the relatively new notion of watching moving pictures was a fun experience, so customers were willing to take their chances. The theater was a marginally profitable business for Carpenter, but by 1916, he had grown restless and had his eye set on taking a road trip—to make money, have fun and promote his Sunshine City hometown.

Carpenter recruited his pal Joe Honey, and together they outfitted a four-cylinder Model 37 Hudson Touring Car with storage chests, supplies and a special cargo area for their six-foot alligator named Trouble. He sold

The sign in the windshield of William Carpenter's car urged approaching motorists to "turn about and follow us to St. Petersburg Florida."

the theater, equipped himself with several boxes of board of trade brochures promoting the city and headed north. The plan was to complete a fourteen-thousand-mile road trip from Florida to New England's coastal villages, through scattered Canadian provinces and on to the vast Rocky Mountains and big-sky states west of the Mississippi River.

Along the way, William and Joe would drop in on friendly looking towns and villages, attract a throng of curiosity seekers and put on a fascinating road show of hypnotizing Trouble. It was Joey's task to solicit orders from onlookers who could have their very own "live baby alligator" shipped directly to them for only $1.50 each. The Hudson served not only as home for Trouble but also as an instant sideshow stage and, on occasion, as bunk space for the two slick promoters. As a rolling billboard, the touring car featured hand-painted messages urging northerners to "Come along to the Sunshine City."

On several occasions, Carpenter had to wire the chamber of commerce (then known as the board of trade) to request a shipment of additional pamphlets to be sent in care of general delivery at his next venue. Sales were good, snowbird interest in experiencing warm Florida winters was piqued and the trip was deemed successful.

Within six months of his tour, several tourists signing in at the visitor's center in St. Petersburg said an alligator road show that they had witnessed in places like Yellowstone Park and Rochester, New York, had convinced them to see what the west coast of Florida had to offer.

The additions Carpenter made to his automobile were not unlike the camping and living modifications many tin can tourists made to their automobiles when they chose to join the hordes of adventurers who would soon flood Florida on the cheap. Many drove Henry's affordable Ford, the Tin Lizzy, but other well-known marques like Hudson, Dodge and Studebaker were driven onto the beaches and into the parks of Florida's villages and towns.

But it wasn't entirely a one-way promotion street. On at least one occasion, a pair of Yankees from Connecticut, intent on having a most excellent road adventure, drove into St. Petersburg in their customized touring sedan. With slogans promoting summer visits to New England, the car's rooftop featured a scale model of the twin lighthouses of Thacher Island on the Massachusetts coast, a road show not nearly as captivating as alligator hypnotics.

The Alligator Man's trip was a success, but after four months on the road, Carpenter longed for home. He returned home just in time for Thanksgiving with a reported $2,000 profit in his wallet.

As for Trouble? Well, reports vary, but the gator also had something to do with wallets—probably ending up as one. And some of those $1.50 baby gators that were shipped to northern customers may have been the basis years later for the popular urban legend of New York City sewers being occupied by the power-jawed beasts. The Alligator Man devoted the remainder of his ninety-plus years to the real estate business, helping to organize and promote the St. Petersburg Board of Realtors.

Frenzied land speculation ensued, subdivisions sprang up and new citizens had homes constructed. Building permits in 1923 alone topped $7 million, while banking deposits soared from just over $2 million in 1916 to over $20 million by the spring of 1924.

The Sunshine City rapidly flourished and experienced more growth in just a few years that would have taken decades to achieve elsewhere. Averaging twelve new citizens a day, the demand for more suitable roads reaching farther into the Pinellas Peninsula quickly arose.

The need to span Tampa Bay eastbound toward Hillsborough County and southward to Manatee County increased with each passing year. New state roads, one from Manatee to Palm Beach and another linking Tampa to Miami, provided more opportunities for tourism and city boosters. St. Petersburg city leaders, determined not to lose dollars deeply buried in the pockets of countless travelers, pushed for bridging Tampa Bay in order to connect Pinellas and these new multilane highways.

Following the Dotted Line

Hailed across the country as a great step forward in development, the late November 1924 opening of Tampa Bay's Gandy Bridge was an instant success. Locally, while nearly thirty thousand people eagerly prepared to turn out for the official ceremony, newspaper headlines boldly proclaimed "St. Petersburg and Tampa United." Amid the "vortex of humanity that crushed together within the structures narrow confines," described one reporter, "a chapter was inscribed Thursday in the book of bridgedom as Gandy Bridge—monarch of spans—was formally dedicated." According to St. Petersburg historian Scott Hartzell, at the dedication ceremony, Gandy's entire speech was four words: "The bridge is built!"

The highly anticipated and much-celebrated toll bridge, nearly six miles in length, joined the booming tourist town of St. Petersburg with Tampa, the industrial- and commercial-driven city across the bay. Although the toll bridge took just two years to construct, George Gandy's vision was

George Gandy (right), fabled to be a man of few words, appears to have captured the attention of C.C. Carr and Eva Alsman Fuller, the wife of Gandy's one-time business partner Walter Fuller, in this candid photo. Carr was an early promoter of bond issues to build brick roads that improved and increased tourist traffic.

two decades in the making and nearly as old as the upstart city of St. Petersburg itself.

Since its inception in June 1888 with the arrival of Peter Demens's Orange Belt Railroad, St. Petersburg had been an aspiring community in the rapidly advancing state of Florida. Nineteenth-century Florida lacked much infrastructure, though. Just a few decades prior to its 1845 entrance into the Union as the twenty-seventh state, swamps, scrublands and Seminoles dominated the Florida scene. As a result, previous attempts to inhabit Florida, seen by many as an absurd adventure into a malaria-infested terrain, proved difficult, if not nearly impossible.

The settling of North America's southernmost landmass came about through legislation and locomotion. In 1842, in accordance with the newly passed Federal Armed Occupation Act, homestead opportunities were available to pioneering people willing to cultivate and physically protect their personal Florida frontier. In addition to the destruction brought about by the 1848 hurricane and then the Civil War, the state's remoteness, swampy sections and general lack of transportation guaranteed sluggish and selective development during the nineteenth century.

Few pioneers had managed the passage to the Gulf Coast, and even fewer witnessed the Orange Belt Railway huff to a stop near the shores of Tampa Bay. Thus was the founding of St. Petersburg.

While their numbers were few and their reasons to relocate to this remote and feral neck of land varied, the pioneering families of St. Petersburg

The original Hotel Detroit can be seen in the background of this turn-of-the-century scene of Orange Belt Railroad locomotive 7 and its crew, circa 1901.

"reflected the restless temperament and enterprising spirit that dominated late nineteenth-century America," noted award-winning author Raymond Arsenault. The same pioneering spirit and determination that drove earlier homesteaders to break new ground on isolated Point Pinellas fueled the actions and accomplishments of St. Petersburg's early twentieth-century boosters and businessmen, such as George Gandy.

Bespectacled and bearded, George Gandy was an impeccably dressed "Victorian looking character," who had arrived in St. Petersburg in 1903. Sensing the potential of the attractive and rapidly growing city, the Gandy family—George, wife Clara and their five children—soon became devoted residents and boosters. Within a decade of his arrival, George Gandy had applied his years of business preparation under the tutelage of a prominent Philadelphia saw manufacturer, Henry Disston, to construct La Plaza Theatre, a magnificent entertainment edifice in the heart of St. Petersburg.

Featuring live performances and movies such as *Birth of a Nation*, Gandy's La Plaza Theatre and office building rapidly became "one of the most beautiful and successful buildings in the history of St. Petersburg, just as its builder envisioned."

Prompted by a promotional map with a dotted line running across the waters of Tampa Bay, George Gandy and local entrepreneur H. Walter Fuller conspired to turn the wishful mark into reality. Although World War I and economic hardships temporarily halted the Gandy and Fuller fantasy, the dream would not fade.

War restrictions on building material and goods, followed by increased supply costs levied after the armistice, often sent investors running or created victims of receivership. H. Walter Fuller, who in his lifetime would earn and lose several fortunes, fell into the latter category. Within a few years after the war's end, George Gandy acquired Fuller's share in the project and began anew. Certainly aware that assistance in raising construction capital was required for such a massive undertaking, Gandy enlisted a silver-tongued northerner to do just that.

Silver Tongues and Satisfied Customers

In the early months of 1922, Eugene Elliot slid into town from New York prepared to pull every trick out of his promoter's hat in order to sell St. Petersburg a bridge. Described by resident Walter Fuller as "the most colorful, tempestuous, super-energized man to ever grace the St. Petersburg stage," Eugene Elliot was just the man for the job. Intense negotiations, wild speculation and impressive skills in oration were nothing new to 1920s Florida. Neither Carl Fisher's sultry Miami Beach nor George Merrick's elegant and exclusive Coral Gables would have materialized without this winning trifecta.

It was no different in St. Petersburg. Within four months' time of his arrival, promoter Eugene Elliot, with an army of smooth-talking salesmen, peddled over $2 million worth of bridge stocks and bonds. To Gandy's delight, bridge construction began by September 1922, the same year that Frank Fortune Pulver tossed his proverbial hat into the political arena for mayor, hoping to "send every tourist back to his home an advertising booster for St. Petersburg," he noted in a letter to the *St. Petersburg Times*.

Frank Fortune Pulver could not have picked a more apropos middle name for himself. "He's got the Midas touch!" an exuberant supporter of the multiterm mayor once said. "Everything he touches turns to gold."

It is true that Pulver was a successful—and wealthy—businessman, who, over the years, was referred to as "the king of chewing gum," "the millionaire mayor," "the flamboyant bachelor'" and "Uncle Frank." However, as it turns out, the Rochester, New York native also possessed one very important quality that may have been directly related to his purported wealth. He knew how to keep his mouth shut.

Pulver came to St. Petersburg in 1918 and quickly developed a reputation as the man who sold William Wrigley Jr. a chewing gum formula for the tidy sum of $1 million. The origin of that saga is unclear, but Frank Fortune Pulver never confirmed nor denied the popular belief (so it must have been true).

Frank Fortune Pulver was said to have the Midas touch.

Even after his death in 1954 at age eighty-four, publications continued to repeat the popular tale that Pulver had obtained his gum formula from a friend for $200, joined forces with his older brother to form the Pulver Chocolate & Chicle Company in Rochester and ultimately sold that formula to Wrigley for the $1 million figure—an intriguing story, but one that is most likely an embellished legend.

At the turn of the century, Pulver—a watchmaker by trade—sold inexpensive jewelry and silverware, using the gum as a sales premium. At one point, he sold some pots to Wrigley, having to personally vouch for the man's creditworthiness before the silverware company would ship the order. The gum incentive was the same type of business model William Wrigley would use himself when, in 1907, he began selling baking powder and giving away sticks of gum as an incentive to buy. The sweet treat, of course, became Wrigley's primary interest.

In reality, the gum business was a sideline for Pulver, an inventor by nature. As dozens of small manufacturers made a variety of gum flavors, Pulver concentrated on dispensing that product. He did not invent the first coin-operated gum machine, but he did create the machines that entertained buyers when they dropped their pennies in the slot. His patent-protected Pulver Gum Machines featured animated figures such as the comic strip character Yellow Kid, bobbing clowns and cops hitting robbers with nightsticks. Most Pulver machines were stocked with three flavors, featuring DiGesto Spearmint along with two less popular flavors. The machines are today very desirable collector's items.

Operating under a variety of New York State corporate names, Pulver was adamant about protecting not only his patent for the animated gum machine but also designs for a perpetual calendar, a film camera–winding device and a waterproof fabric. Older brother Henry also had an inventive bent and secured several U.S. patents to the original Pulver machine. Nothing relating to a gum formula deal with William Wrigley can be found in archived New York State public records.

Their deal had nothing to do with how gum was *made*, but rather how it was marketed and trademarked.

The book *William Wrigley, Jr.: The Man and His Business, 1861–1932*, is today the preferred reference source used by customer service and media representatives at the Wm. Wrigley Jr. Company to document the history of the Illinois-based gum empire. Author William Zimmerman says the company has no record of a formula purchase agreement between Pulver and Wrigley. However, that does not mean Pulver didn't profit from a deal involving the spearmint name and trademarks.

An obscure volume of the *1919 Federal Court Reporter*, detailing decisions reached by the U.S. Seventh Circuit Court and the appellate court, sheds new light on Pulver's wealth and reveals the Wrigley court battle was over the use of the word "spearmint," not a gum formula.

As soon as William Wrigley Jr. recognized that his gum was more popular than his baking powder, he moved full speed ahead in the gum business. His philosophy for success was simple: "tell 'em quick and tell 'em often." He advertised on a grand scale, on buses and streetcars, on benches, billboards and baseball stadiums. At one point, he mailed three sticks of gum to each of the 1.5 million names in the phone directory. According to biographer Zimmerman, the gum salesman fiercely defended his product name and image, frequently defeating his would-be competitors in the courtroom. That is precisely what happened with Frank Pulver.

Volume 253 of the *Federal Reporter* summarizes lawsuits between Wrigley and a competing gum manufacturer named Larson. Their particular fight was over trademark infringements and the use of the names "spearmint," "peptomint" and "wintergreen." An excerpt of the court ruling explains common industry practices:

> *In gum making before Wrigley's time it was common practice to form (gum) sticks of the size and shape now used by Wrigley; to wrap the sticks in pink paper; to put 5 sticks in a package; to put 20 packages in a box; to tie each package of 5 pink sticks with a counter band of white paper; to use red and green printers' inks on the white counter band…(and to) display the maker's name and "Gum" or "Pepsin Gum" in red letters.*

To support its *Larson v. Wrigley* decision, the Seventh Circuit Court of Appeals cited an earlier decree involving Pulver and Wrigley—an agreed-to settlement that remained virtually unknown and certainly unpublicized:

> *Wrigley was not the first to apply "Spearmint" as a display word of special emphasis. That had been done by Pulver years before Wrigley came on the scene. So there was nothing that Wrigley did not take from others, except his own name and the spear as the design on which to spread the word "Spearmint." Wrigley, of course, knew these facts, and also the inside story of his suit against Pulver.*

As explained by the *Federal Reporter*, the court order divulges exactly how Pulver quietly accumulated some of his wealth from Wrigley:

> *According to the final decree in that case, Wrigley, not Pulver, was the originator of the "Spearmint" package. But the decree was not entered until Wrigley owned both sides of the lawsuit; He gave Pulver $100,000 in cash and $150,000 in notes running one to five years. If Pulver should fail to keep still, there might be trouble in collecting the notes remaining unpaid.*

Clearly, Frank Pulver knew the value of keeping quiet, so he was apparently more than willing to let the "gum millionaire" stories circulate unconfirmed and uncontested. There is no doubt that he was wealthy; it's just that the money in Frank Fortune Pulver's pockets did not necessarily all come from William Wrigley Jr.

After seeing just one publicity photograph of St. Petersburg's flamboyant millionaire mayor decked out in his trademark white suit and Panama hat, it makes perfect sense that he would invest some of his time and fortune in the laundry business. After all, white suits show dirt. For brief periods, the three-term mayor also owned the Hotel Detroit, the city's first; the toll bridge to Pass-a-Grille; and the *Daily News* newspaper.

Serving as mayor and as the official bathing suit inspector was a tough job, but "the millionaire bachelor" was willing to accept the challenge as he strolled past curious onlookers with a bevy of temptresses.

The white suit was made famous by John Lodwick's creation of the "Purity League" and Pulver pictured at various "official" scanty bathing suit inspections.

One reporter wrote that Pulver wore the readily identifiable white suit attire year-round. The news sleuth claimed that during colder months or on visits to his New York hometown stomping grounds of Rochester, Pulver donned red flannel long johns underneath his "uniform." There don't seem to be any Lodwick photos in existence that prove or disprove this claim. At the opening of the 1922 World Horseshoe Championships—brought to St. Petersburg by none other than John Lodwick—the pair of promoters provided opening-day entertainment as described by historian Gary Kline:

> *At opening ceremonies, John Lodwick, World Tournament Publicity Manager, placed his new straw Mackin hat on the stake. He then dared Mayor Frank Fortune Pulver, whose attire included white shoes and straw hat, to hit it. Of four shoes thrown, 18 inches was as close as he got.*

Spectators filled the bleachers of Sunshine Park for "World Championship Horse Shoe Pitching" brought to St. Petersburg through the creative promotional genius of John Lodwick.

Pulver's white suit in later years struck a chord with the Jaycees. Whether it was the intent of these young civic leaders to pay homage to Pulver or to simply have fun, they initiated an annual "white suit day." Usually during the last week in May, they urged residents and visitors alike to deck themselves out in straw hats and their best springtime white garb.

In 1923, Pulver organized the commercial laundries in town to form Chatauqua Laundry, renamed one year later as the Soft Water Laundry, Inc. He hired Russell M. Knightly to oversee the day-to-day operations of the company, but the controversial mayor/publicity hound/inventor/businessman retained control of the company until his death. During World War II, Knightly hit on the idea of providing laundry service to the hundreds of military men who were living throughout the city in hotels that had been taken over by the War Department as military housing. These were patriotic times of conservation, and laundry facilities frequently bought back wire hangers from their customers for a penny each.

Called simply "Uncle Frank" by many of his employees, Pulver was known for enforcing a strict work ethic, but he was also generous with rewards. He frequently gave out bonuses and would stage elaborate family picnics even during periods of peak business. Managers and supervisors served as cooks and bottle washers for these family-style thank-you fests. At Christmas, every Pulver employee received a fruit basket, turkey and all

Proclaiming to be the bright spot in the Sunshine City, this Hotel Detroit postcard was aimed specifically at residents in Chicago and New York.

the necessary holiday feast trimmings. At its height in the mid-1950s, the Soft Water Laundry employed three hundred people, who worked seven days a week, and produced annual sales in excess of $1 million. Several disputes with the National Labor Relations Board and various unions erupted, but the company held on, with Pulver surprisingly remaining in the background. By the mid-1980s, mechanization had begun to take over, giant one-thousand-pound-capacity washing machines and water extractors reduced the total workforce to about eighty employees. All of the laundry's business was directed toward the commercial hotel and restaurant markets with family accounts no longer on the books. Sheets, towels and uniforms for hospitals also became part of the operation, with the laundry owning about 90 percent of the inventory.

His knowledge of the laundry business inspired Pulver to sketch out another notable invention. In 1945, he received patent number 2378789 for a continuous-roll towel-dispensing machine, which for twenty years was a common public-hygiene device in gas station and restaurant restrooms across the country. Of course, the rolls of soiled cloth towels had to be commercially cleaned, resulting in more business for his laundry.

Armed with an appreciation for advertising and a bankroll to boost, the "millionaire bachelor" soon became one of the city's "invaluable men of visions," wrote *St. Petersburg Times* columnist Dick Bothwell, "anxious to put the power of advertising behind the town's bandwagon." Spreading the message in full-page ads, Pulver spent thousands upon thousands of dollars highlighting St. Petersburg in northern newspapers.

Seven hundred miles away, in 1905, another natural-born salesman—all of nine years old—hawked newspapers for Nashville's largest daily, the *Tennessean*. Soon, James Webb was managing a crew of fourteen other newsies and was making a whopping eight dollars monthly. Always wanting to offer the customer more, Webb began selling hot German bread to his customers three days a week. His family had a garden and a cow, so he started selling vegetables and milk. Not one to sit still, the youngster mowed lawns and sold lemonade at a curbside stand. He took the unsold juice and made sherbet for the next day's customers. At the ripe age of twelve, Webb decided he was too busy for school and dropped out of the fifth grade. That same year, the family relocated to Knoxville, where Webb promptly found work setting pins at a bowling alley, working the soda fountain and helping around a local pharmacy, Economy Drug Company.

By age twenty, Webb had married and become manager and part owner of the drugstore. It was here that James Webb earned a lifelong nickname as "Doc." That moniker fit the slight five-foot-five man, as he was always testing and marketing quick-cure remedies and elixirs. Without license requirements or FDA interference, pharmacists like Doc took advantage of the lack of regulation on patent medicines. Soon, he began selling his cure-all "Doc Webb's 608." Primarily intended to treat gonorrhea, the concoction was little more than \$0.70 worth of gum acacia and sandalwood. He sold it for \$5.50 a bottle. It sold like hotcakes. In a few years, that experience would ultimately prove itself in St. Petersburg.

Leaflets and Postcards

William Alexander Holshouser was one of the twelve original founders of the St. Petersburg Board of Trade, serving as its first president in 1903. He was an enthusiastic advocate of promoting patent medicines and advertising the benefits of living in his beloved Tampa Bay town. His pharmacy operated from a small Central Avenue storefront, more or less in the center of the main business district of the small town. In addition to dispensing castor oil and Epsom salts, Holshouser produced leaflets that would fit into a standard-

An early postcard view of properly dressed men and women fishing in the sleepy little village of St. Petersburg.

size envelope. He gave these brochures to his customers and urged them to mail the flyers to friends in the north, inviting them to visit St. Petersburg.

The gist of his message was that the Pinellas Peninsula was indeed exactly what Dr. Van Bibber, a late nineteenth-century physician, had claimed it to be: "the healthiest place in the country." Being a good businessman, his flyers also promoted a "guaranteed" formula that he claimed would totally eliminate dandruff in just two weeks. The genius of Holshouser's scheme was that his customers incurred almost all the promotion cost and effort: they identified the potential visitors, provided the envelopes and paid the postage. Oh, and his drugstore just happened to sell envelopes, too.

By all accounts, his tourist promotion efforts produced better results than the antiflake compound. Thanks to his direct mail success, Holshouser was later instrumental in the first publication of ten thousand city booklets at a cost of $125. In 1905, he asked city leaders for $500 to print additional copies, and they turned him down, calling the request "frivolous." But Holshouser continued schemes to attract folks to his beloved paradise.

In 1915, when the Philadelphia Phillies won their first National League baseball championship in thirty-two years, Holshouser helped spearhead a creative way for fans living in St. Petersburg to kill three birds with one stone. The savvy pharmacist/promoter wanted to congratulate the team, thank them for choosing the Sunshine City as their spring training site and advertise his city to northerners—all in one fell swoop.

Instead of a ticker tape parade, he hit on the idea of urging local residents to write congratulatory messages and accolades on postcards that would then be scattered in the air during the Phillies' hometown pennant victory parade. (Once again, the penny postcards just happened to be available at his drugstore.) The picture postcards promoting life in a sun-filled playground were shipped in bulk to Phils' manager Pat Moran so he could arrange to have them thrown from windows along the downtown Philadelphia parade route. One card featured in the local newspaper had this original fan message:

A foxy geezer is old Patrick Moran.
To all other managers, he's tied a can:
He put sand in each player's shoes,
and then lead them to it—they just couldn't lose.

The poetry may be lacking, but the enthusiasm was there. The Phillies put up an impressive fight against Boston but ultimately lost the 1915 World

Series to the home run–hammering Red Sox. Nevertheless, St. Petersburg residents and visitors alike swarmed to spring training the following year, spending money. But Philadelphia reverted to what might be called a perennial slump, failing to take another pennant for sixty-five years and never again experiencing another St. Petersburg postcard blitz.

It was Holshouser's board of trade that would take a leap of faith and hire John Lodwick, the ambitious Ohio sportswriter, as the first public relations person for any American city.

A Deal They Couldn't Refuse

The first major attempt at advertising the city, in 1913, cost the St. Petersburg Board of Trade $4,000 for fifty thousand copies of an enticing sixteen-page illustrated folder. Early and less elaborate efforts came in postcard form. One illustrated postcard produced after the successful 1905–06 tourist season featured sightseers and fishing visitors enjoying the ample aquatic life on the city's extensive waterfront. Unquestionably, the solicitation tempted tourists to discover Pinellas Point: "For the Best Winter and Summer Climate on Earth Come to St. Petersburg By-the-Gulf-Stream…The Tourist Paradise…The Homeseeker's Refuge…The Land of Now and the Country of Splendid Realities."

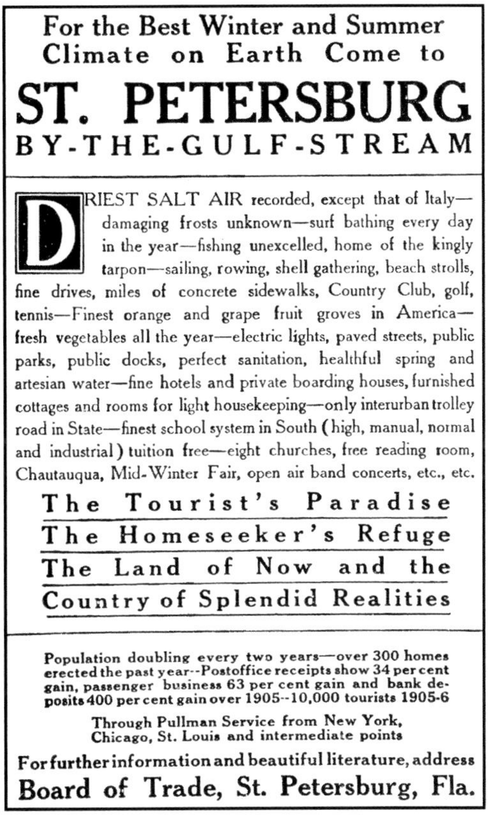

Hyperbole at its best in this board of trade handout promoting "the best winter and summer climate on earth."

In 1920, St. Petersburg's board of trade formally

changed its name to the chamber of commerce. The organization was so instrumental to St. Petersburg's success, wrote Karl Grismer in 1948, that "to relate the activities of the Chamber since 1920 would be like repeating the history of the city." Since the group's origination in 1899, the board/chamber brought about "countless ways to make St. Petersburg a finer place to live."

Some schemes to promote St. Petersburg and its tourism industry worked far better than others. After reading a 1924 newspaper story about how tiring it was for travelers to wait in lines to sign in at busy hotels, one entrepreneur had an idea for travelers from St. Petersburg who might experience similar sign-in slowdowns in northern states.

St. Petersburg car salesman Vaughn Getts purchased a rubber stamp with his signature and address in bold letters so he could quickly and clearly sign any guest register. Because his hometown of "ST. PETERSBURG, FLA." was so legible, it caught the eye of others who would invariably ask questions about the Sunshine City and about the stamp. A great way, Getts claimed, to be an "ambassador of our hometown." But the idea never quite took hold, probably because the stamp was just one more thing to forget when packing for a trip.

Even municipal engineers got in on the act of promoting St. Petersburg to the rest of the world. In 1924, Robert E. Ludwig, the director of public works, wrote a lengthy story about the city's new "white way" street-lighting system, then being installed by the General Electric Company. Three professional publications, *American City*, *Electrical World* and *American Municipalities* all published his article in addition to printing ads purchased by GE. More than forty-eight thousand city officials and engineers across the United States read about the "modern advancements" of St. Petersburg. Always looking for a superlative to tag onto a story, it was asserted that the street electrification system was the longest white way in the world.

In addition to successfully advocating municipal improvements, the chamber of commerce organized local civic clubs and social groups for visiting vacationers, promoting the city continuously and countrywide. The board of trade's best investment, however, was in John Lodwick.

A few months before board of trade president Charles Carter championed for an unprecedented $20,000 to advertise St. Petersburg during the 1918–19 tourist season, the city retained the services of John Lodwick, at no charge. "I'll do the job," the fast-talking newcomer from Ohio informed board secretary L.A. Whitney, "and at the end of the season you pay me what you think it has been worth."

Central Avenue with its famous green benches was christened as a progressive "white way" with the early installation of General Electric street lighting.

Lodwick's cut-rate price and lofty goals for putting St. Petersburg in the lexicon of southbound tourists sealed the deal. Whitney hired Lodwick as the city's first publicity director on the spot.

John Lodwick, who had come to Florida via Cleveland, worked for several years promoting sporting events in his home state. With a penchant for writing and a need for the healing rays of Tampa Bay, Lodwick soon settled in to a freelance-reporting gig with the *St. Petersburg Times*. It was through Walter Fuller, a staffwriter for the newspaper at the time, that Lodwick happened upon L.A. Whitney.

His grand scheme, Lodwick informed Whitney and Fuller over lunch, was to turn St. Petersburg into a sporting capital, hosting a multitude of "world championships" throughout the year. The publicity, he insisted, would reach national audiences free of charge.

The ultimate goal in this plan was to create headlines and datelines displaying "St. Petersburg, Florida" in publications from Peoria to Portland, featuring Tampa Bay's natural beauty and ideal climate as a backdrop for every story. While battling the chilly winds of yet another northern blizzard, Lodwick first conceived of working in Pinellas's propaganda department several years prior and knew of the Sunshine State's siren call. For Lodwick, "Florida's sun beckoned," reminisced a local journalist in 1938.

"Parasol Pretty" and "Beauty and the Beach" were just a couple of the captions used by travel magazines and newspapers that published this Lodwick technique photo.

John Lodwick's showmanship and insatiable ability to create sensational situations made his first season in St. Petersburg a huge success. Coupled with the board of trade's extensive advertising campaign throughout Florida, John Lodwick's skill sealed the city's popularity for the following tourist season as well.

"Naturally, the best manner of selling St. Petersburg's sunshine was through the medium of the pretty girl," disclosed columnist Jane Graham on the topic of bathing beauties, and John Lodwick became master of the medium. Although Miami Beach's Carl Fisher gave birth to the "Bathing Beauties," which soon became that city's trademark, St. Petersburg boosters took the scantily clad sea-nymph theme in a new direction. Through a mix of practical jokes and pure sensationalism, propaganda guru John Lodwick and Mayor Pulver devised the St. Petersburg Purity League.

The spurious organization felt it its duty to extend the league's puritanical values to St. Petersburg's shores. Supposedly outraged at the nearly nude nubile woman parading on the sandy playgrounds in their newfangled one-piece suits, Purity "members" insisted on moral enforcements and inspections, and the mayor was very happy to oblige. As planned, word of the swimsuit shakedown made national news.

In a classic example of feeding the press, boosters must have stifled a snicker as they sent the wire northward:

> *Florida Purity League Moves*
> *"To Protect the Married Men."*
> *ST. PETERSBURG, Fla., Jan 25—Mayor Frank Pulver had a request today from the St. Petersburg Purity League that he appoint a bathing suit inspector, a formal communications from the organization stating that "the league intends to protect the married men from the wiles of the sea vamp." The Mayor said he would personally visit the beach and look 'em over.*
>
> —Reno Evening Gazette, *Jan. 25, 1922*

Aside from such publicity pranks while in office, Pulver performed his greatest act of boosterism after his stint as mayor had ended. In January 1924, amid frantic growth, a new city charter and much opinionated mudslinging, Pulver was recalled from his post as mayor. Ironically, like his predecessor and fellow civic booster Noel Mitchell, Pulver had performed great services for the city's image and infrastructure only to be a victim of fair-weather citizens' whims and worries.

Shortly thereafter, Pulver, who now had plenty of free time to go with his fortune, left St. Petersburg on a four-month whirlwind worldwide promotional tour. Dressed in his usual snowy white suit and white-brimmed hat, Pulver traveled nearly twenty thousand miles extolling the ecstasies of St. Petersburg. His journey eventually took him to Buckingham Palace, where he met King George and the queen.

Always the pitchman, Pulver claimed to have cornered the Prince of Wales in the lovely ten-acre Royal Gardens. Upon shaking the prince's hand, Pulver suggested that the prince tour St. Petersburg on his next visit to America. The prince smiled and replied, "I think it would be rather warm there at this season of the year. I would like to visit Florida in the wintertime."

Pulver's publicity junket had worked. Newspapers nationwide ran stories of the "Man in White," his brazen boasts of the Sunshine State and Pulver's invitation for all to visit Florida's west coast wonderland, St. Petersburg. Frank Pulver returned to his beloved city in the summer of 1924.

During Pulver's absence, John Lodwick and the chamber of commerce were busy securing St. Petersburg's future. "In fact," an April announcement agreed, "several of the most important projects so far as the future growth of greater St. Petersburg is concerned were launched."

Civic matters ranged from railroad improvements and relocating water traffic to the Bayboro Harbor to a toll-free beach causeway proposal and plans for a new downtown recreational pier.

In 1924, W.B. Sanders, editor of the *Nunda News* in Livingston County, New York, summed up the entire St. Petersburg success philosophy with a front-page "Travel Letter" to his subscribers:

> *What is sending St. Petersburg ahead is the solid community spirit.*
>
> *Everybody believes in the man who believes in himself. St. Petersburg believes in itself, talks, writes and advertises the city at every turn, and the permanent residents are all united in sounding its praises and co-operating to prove the soundness of their judgment to others.*

In addition to purchasing a Pullman railcar and printing 200,000 small booklets to advertise the Sunshine City and the Royal Scotch Highlanders Band, a beloved group that drew thousands to Williams Park, the chamber ran display advertisements in various boating publications and prepared nearly 250,000 brochures for general use. The high-demand brochures, reported the *Chamber of Commerce Bulletin for May 1924*, "containing much

Thousands of postcards promoting the Gandy Bridge as a modern-day wonder of the world brought new fame and tourists' dollars to the Tampa Bay area.

more attractive matter than any previous city booklet," would be one of the final promotional pieces featuring a bridgeless bay.

Had Frank F. Pulver waited a few more months to return from his goodwill mission selling St. Petersburg, the former mayor may have been among the first to hand over seventy-five cents and cross Tampa Bay by automobile on Gandy's grand bridge.

In November 1924, at a cost of $3 million and just over two years of construction, the Gandy Bridge was completed.

Governors and public officials from twenty-five states partook in the dedication. It truly was a marvel to behold. Around 1,500 construction workers, using dredges and donkeys, among other tools of the day, constructed three miles of sand-filled causeways. In between the land bridges, two and a half miles of reinforced concrete soared over Tampa Bay. Shaving the commuter time from forty-three minutes to nineteen, Gandy's "world's longest toll-road and bridge" put St. Petersburg on the map and literally connected the city to the rest of Florida.

"More than any other single development," notes southern historian Raymond Arsenault, "the opening of the Gandy Bridge was responsible for raising the (land) boom to it dizzying apogee of 1925."

Land between downtown St. Petersburg and Gandy's span, once deemed undesirable property, sold at skyrocketing prices. Subdivisions and storefronts soon sprouted along the major corridors connecting the city center to the highly anticipated overpass.

The bridging of Tampa Bay, publicized in movies, magazines and monthly periodicals around the globe, was just the boost the Sunshine City needed. The faster direct route into St. Petersburg and its benefits to the traveler were obvious; but for city boosters, who for years had "preached a civic religion that proclaimed the wonders of Florida—and their hometown specifically," St. Petersburg was their version of the Promised Land.

"All they needed to make their heaven last," wrote Professor Bruce Stephenson in his probing works *Visions of Eden: Environmentalism, Urban Planning, and City Building in St. Petersburg, Florida,* "was to lead others there."

Gandy and his toll bridge became the messiahs of this message.

By December 1925, local chamber of commerce display advertisements sent to newspapers nationally featured the Gandy Bridge while reminding readers that St. Petersburg, "on sunny Pinellas Peninsula between the broad Gulf of Mexico and Tampa Bay," offered a "wonderful winter playground where every desire for outdoor sports and recreation can be fulfilled." Readers of the December 13, 1925 *New York Times* surely must have shivered just a bit more after seeing those ads. St. Petersburg could not have devised a better public relation success story or a better route to usher in tourists.

Advertising executives might argue the point, but there is little question that word of mouth is one of the most powerful tools in gaining—or losing—customers. No matter what product or service one may be trying to sell, a personal reference, warning or recommendation carries a lot of weight. And in the world of promotion, an unsolicited written testimony of praise is golden, as evidenced by modern-day sellers who routinely urge their customers to write Internet reviews and ratings.

At the turn of the twentieth century, his name wasn't a household word, nor were there volumes written about him, but Colonel John H. Shanklin of Trenton, Missouri, deserves at least some credit for selling St. Petersburg. In fact, historian, developer, legislator, promoter and newspaperman Walter P. Fuller asserted in his book *St. Petersburg and Its People* that Shanklin deserves to be recognized as "the first official tourist" to the Sunshine City. Fuller concedes that other visitors no doubt preceded Shanklin, but Fuller says the retired lawyer was the first tourist to document his first and subsequent pilgrimages to St. Petersburg. And just like government work or military training, the job of promotion isn't considered complete without the paperwork.

So enamored by the pleasant climate and the bountiful fishing, Shanklin wrote daily accounts of his winter seasons in Florida, sending them back home to the Grundy County newspaper for regular publication. As a practicing attorney, he had been a frequent contributor to the *Missouri Central Law Journal*, building a reputation as a convincing communicator. His writings were marked by "strong, clear, vigorous statements," writes Missouri historian J.D. Stewart in a biography of the lawyer, adding, "his analysis, logic and conclusions therefore seemed irresistible." Stewart goes on to laud Shanklin as delivering in 1883 the "best annual address ever presented" to the Missouri Bar Association.

After forty years of being "a student of law," as he was fond of saying, Shanklin retired and began traveling. He painstakingly documented his journeys: "Departure time from Trenton, 4:00 p.m., January 1, 1893; Arrived St. Petersburg the afternoon of January 9, following a short stopover in St. Augustine."

From that point on, the Mexican War veteran couldn't stop writing about the west coast of Florida, especially St. Petersburg and its then home county of Hillsborough. In 1895, he published a forty-eight-page collection of his letters to friends back in Grundy County, proclaiming that no other locale was "more abundantly congenial to health and comfort" than the Pinellas Peninsula. A second, slightly larger booklet entitled *Additional Off-hand Shots from Florida* soon followed and was serialized in his show-me hometown newspaper.

Fuller wrote that the Shanklin essays attracted dozens of newcomers to the area and spread the health-city gospel. In 1972, Fuller argued that a memorial should be erected in one of St. Peterburg's city parks, giving full credit to the Missouri lawyer as the "First Official Tourist" because "he had the paperwork to prove it."

A Mother's Breakfast

While the connection of two great cities, Tampa and St. Petersburg, permeated national newspapers in late 1924, their separation a few years prior had made countless more headlines, at least in Florida. Neither sensational advertisements nor strategically placed editorials held up to the praise heaped on St. Petersburg from the writings and ranting of William Lincoln Straub.

Part owner and editor of the *St. Petersburg Times*, William Straub had a perfect pulpit. During his nearly four-decade tenure (1901–39), save for a few years in between as postmaster, Straub rarely overlooked the opportunity to push for St. Petersburg's prosperity.

"I came here to die," William Straub proclaimed in a 1932 *Times* editorial; instead, he "found health in St. Petersburg." Statements such as these were far from rare; however, few said it to so many, and fewer said it so often.

William Straub came to Florida a wearied man battling recurring bronchitis as the twentieth century rapidly approached. Unwilling to leave North Dakota and return to his native state of Michigan to recuperate while avoiding doctor's orders to operate, Straub headed to the Sunshine State.

Within weeks of reading, resting and walking in St. Petersburg's therapeutic sunrays, he found that his bronchitis had all but disappeared. From that day forward, Straub was convinced of the tiny fishing hamlet's offerings. However, St. Petersburg was not his first stop in the bay area—Tampa was.

Unfortunately for the city of Tampa, Straub's first impressions of the "Cigar Capital of the World" were not happy ones.

"It was a disappointment," he said of the former base of operations for the Spanish-American War. "No paving, no cleanliness, no nothing."

Crossing Tampa Bay, William Straub found in St. Petersburg all that postwar Tampa lacked: pristine beaches, clean water and even "breakfast like mother made." In a short time, he secured part ownership of the *St. Petersburg Times*, beginning a lifelong crusade.

From his home and downtown office, William Straub worked incessantly to advance his newly adopted city. Some say he introduced one of the first promotion pieces of advertising for the city in 1903. Rather artistic, Straub created a spectacular—and fictitious—painting of downtown St. Petersburg's waterfront.

Gone were the current worn-out wharves and other derelict harbor-edge eyesores; in their places stood stately structures and picturesque piers lined with luxurious steamboats. Straub had painted a panoramic view of what could be. Painted for Frank A. Davis, the owner of St. Petersburg's power company, the work soon hung on a wall of the Pennsylvania Railroad Station.

A simpler line drawing of the same scene became the *St. Petersburg Times* official masthead. Always the astute businessman, Davis, a former Philadelphian, shrewdly shared in Straub's vision and desire to lure northern tourists and citizens to the Sunshine City.

This idyllic waterfront vista, painted by William Straub, was an exercise in virtual reality and became the basic design for the *St. Petersburg Times* newspaper's masthead. Straub painted the vision he had in his mind's eye of what the waterfront could be, not as it actually was.

As the wishful painting reflected, William Straub visualized a city void of beached boats, ramshackle fishing huts dotting the shore and warehouses emitting their noxious fumes. "Leave that to Tampa and Key West," wrote Morton Polk in the *Times*. A city of public parks bordering the bay, for all to enjoy, became Straub's mantra. He envisioned a day when the Pinellas Peninsula politically separated from Hillsborough to become its own county. Straub rarely spared ink or column inches to spread his visions in the *St. Petersburg Times*.

The *Times*'s flair for promoting its namesake city, however, preceded William Straub and his engaging editorials of "peerless Pinellas." As early as 1899, *Times* headlines pronounced St. Petersburg "The Ideal City by the Sea" where "broad avenues, fine driveways and bicycle paths" ran alongside elegant hotels and beautiful residences. No other place in the Sunshine State, the *Times* insisted, offered finer fishing, better boating or more congenial climates than St. Petersburg.

In less than a decade since the Orange Belt Railroad opened Pinellas to dreamers and schemers, civic boosters and copy editors realized the power of the testimonial.

"Tourists tell us," the late nineteenth-century commentary continues, "that for beauty of buildings and location, and as a health resort, there is not a rival in the State of Florida."

God's Resting Place and Buried Treasure

In 1911, William Straub, obviously needing a break from the soapbox and the pressures of politics, and perhaps as a silent reward to himself for his lengthy legislative success, began construction on the family beach hideaway and summer cottage.

Located on St. Petersburg's gulf islands, Straub's Loafer Lodge sat on the southern portion of Long Key. The lodge's construction in the community of Pass-a-Grille superseded sidewalks and streets. "It was one of the first houses," penned daughter Blanche some years after.

"That was before there was any electricity or—well, there was no town at all," she said. Getting to the island required a lesson in logistics. Taking a streetcar to the southern portion of the peninsula, the family would hire a captain and boat across Boca Ciega Bay, eventually disembarking on the southern tip of the barrier island. What they did not, or could not, purchase at Captain Merry's pier had to be brought from the mainland.

"I don't know how my mother ever managed," Blanche confessed, "but she took groceries, bedding—everything, even ice. Of course, the ice didn't last long." Once there, however, visitors eagerly soaked up the sunshine, strung a fishing line from the pier or simply enjoyed the serenity.

Within a few years of Loafer Lodge's debut, the new Pass-a-Grille ferry navigated Boca Ciega Bay, thereby eliminating, or at least reducing, some of the challenges of a beach outing. Although the shuttle service received fanfare for its convenience, the islands desperately needed an automobile

The land of fruit and flowers didn't actually look that appealing in this promotional postcard, but it helped attract investors and land speculators during the Florida boom years.

bridge to bring about any serious development to Long Key. William Straub now had a new soapbox on which to stand.

The closing of the Florida Seminole Wars in 1857 ushered in Long Key's "resort debut." Wishing to wash away the sins of war, or perhaps more interested in the abundant fishing and wild game, local soldiers and the adventurous sought out Long Key. Soon, local schooner pilot Juan (John) Gomez shuttled picnickers and promoters to the key.

Gomez, a self-declared pirate and an originator of Tampa Bay fiction, created and promoted rich tales to entertain his passengers. He enjoyed expounding on Tampa Bay's endowments, reportedly informing one of the area's first white settlers, Dr. Odet Phillipi, "If there is a God, surely this is His resting place."

Gomez enjoyed a good yarn as well. One of his most outlandish fables places him aboard the boat of buccaneer and all-around bad boy Jose Gaspar. Pirates or not, Long Key had become a treasure in its own right. Despite Gomez's sensational stories, Long Key's Pass-a-Grille is one of Florida's, and certainly St. Petersburg's, oldest island resort communities.

The modernization of Pinellas and its Gulf islands from a wild, untamed and unspoiled terrain owes its impetus to the push for "progress" and "development."

Throughout Florida's mainland, fifty dollars could get an enterprising soul forty acres, free and clear. For much less money, wrote Eunice Beecher in her 1879 *Letters from Florida*, sweat equity and fifteen dollars secured a quarter section of government land with the provisions that taxes would be waived for five years "or long enough to bring the land into a state of cultivation." However, one must not be afraid to work very hard for very little, Harriet Beecher Stowe's sister-in-law continues, for "they will find abundant need of all their energies in improving their own land.

For the Pinellas vacationer, however, the United States Railroad Administration assured those coming to the lovely city in 1919 that St. Petersburg's Gulf beaches were accessible by a new automobile bridge and that "the great number of bright, sunny days and its genial climate make it especially agreeable to those who seek rest and recuperation." St. Petersburg, the guidebook championed, "is essentially a winter home resort, and is the center of a colony of northern people who have built beautiful cottages, and who have established here a charming social life under ideal conditions."

As that "great and noble experiment" of Prohibition was finding its way to Pinellas County, bridging the barrier islands to the mainland topped the agenda of both civic leaders and developers. Owner of five hundred acres on the northern portion of Long Key, William McAdoo hired a St. Petersburg's Municipal Pier contractor to span Boca Ciega Bay and connect the island to mainland St. Petersburg. Running two lanes from the west shore of St. Petersburg, at Villa Grande Avenue, motorists on William McAdoo's bridge would disembark at today's Eighty-seventh Avenue on Long Key.

The wood-slatted, rickety construction, toll and all, connected St. Petersburg to McAdoo's new project, St. Petersburg Beach. Despite complaints that "he charged a toll and operated at his whim," said Jari Mogavero, site coordinator of the Gulf Beaches Historical Museum in Pass-a-Grille, McAdoo's bridge was a great achievement for local tourism and travelers bound for the barrier islands.

Local historian and land developer Frank Hurley Jr. shared an entertaining tale of William McAdoo's attempt to sell his grand plan of a seaside attraction on the small island. The story deals with boomtime antics and buried treasure.

Bordering McAdoo's holding was another small barrier island to the north. With the help of a few accomplices and a sturdy wagon, William McAdoo devised a devious plan to make headlines for his beach assets. In the stealth of night, McAdoo buried a large wooden chest loaded with lead weights near the water's edge. The following morning, ensuring that several tourists were in view to witness the "discovery," William McAdoo and his crew removed the "treasure," loading it on a drawn wagon. With McAdoo driving and his shotgun-brandishing partners protecting their find, the trio headed into St. Petersburg, where the "treasure chest" took center stage in the front window of a local downtown bank.

The modern-day pirate's plan backfired. An incorrect account soon spread that the chest had been unearthed on the island adjacent to McAdoo's St. Petersburg Beach, stripping the island of a tall tale and permanently labeling the key to the north "Treasure Island."

Although the Pinellas barrier islands have a long, rich history of settlers, "real development," wrote Karl Grismer in *The Story of St. Petersburg*, "began with the completion of the bridge." No longer required to secure passage aboard a vessel to visit infamous Pass-a-Grille, Sunday drivers and winter residents welcomed the span. They turned out in droves to visit pristine beaches, supped on fifty-cent seaside smorgasbords and gawked at Thomas Rowe's impressive Don CeSar Hotel.

Erected at a cost of $1.5 million and named for a renowned opera, Rowe's Don CeSar added "another big attraction to the Sunshine City as the largest and most magnificent hotel on the Gulf of Mexico." As Pass-a-Grille became

Right: An army air corps airman relaxes in a beachside lifeguard chair while recuperating from what was then known as "battle fatigue." The majestic Don CeSar, nicknamed the Flak Hotel, served the military as a major treatment and observation center for combat stress disorders.

Below: One of America's most famous couples, during both marriage and divorce, Marilyn Monroe and Joe DiMaggio were among the rich and famous to relax on the Don's private beach.

"an important center of social life," Thomas Rowe's towering pink stucco and stone hotel, "the Don," became a playground for the rich and famous and those seeking rest and relaxation during the war years.

On the Right Track

A.A. Stebbins proposed the idea of buying a Pullman sleeper coach in 1924 as a unique and mobile way of promoting the city. Stebbins, who might be called a nostalgic progressive, sold his fellow realty board members on his idea by reminiscing about "the good old days" and the excitement that arose when the circus came to town. "Everybody in town wanted to see the railcars, animals and performers. It was exciting," he argued. A Pullman car decorated to depict the beauty of St. Petersburg and transporting a popular vaudeville show and band around the country would generate the same kind of anticipation as a circus arrival. The city already had a contract with Roy D. Smith and his Royal Scotch Highlanders Band for a season of afternoon and evening concerts in Williams Park. In the off-season summer months, the troupe traveled north for a series of roadshows. Stebbins predicted that providing the Scotch Highlanders with upscale Pullman-car transportation would be an ideal attraction to draw more tourists to St. Petersburg.

He put his money where his mouth was and kicked in the first $1,000 toward buying the luxury coach. The eighty-foot-long Pullman had originally been built at a cost of nearly $40,000, but the group of real estate men managed to obtain it for $15,000. As with many fund drives, however, there were some hiccups in the plan that delayed the use of the railcar. Stebbins refused to turn over ownership of the Pullman to the chamber of commerce until it was paid for in full. "We aren't going to saddle them with a debt that will benefit us the most by attracting new land buyers to our city," he declared. The public agreed, and the balance was quickly paid off by contributions from more than one hundred private citizens and businesses. Some donated materials to refurbish and decorate the car. A light gray paint, appropriately named St. Petersburg Gray, was specifically formulated for the project. The Pullman was topped off with a blue roof and six-inch-high gold lettering proclaiming, "ST. PETERSBURG, FLORIDA, THE SUNSHINE CITY." Members of the local art club, guided by Edith Tadd Little and Paul Conant, decorated the inside of the sleeper with paintings and photographs of various Sunshine City landmarks.

The "band that made St. Petersburg famous," director Roy D. Smith and his Royal Scotch Highlanders, performed free daily concerts in Williams Park as part of its contract with the city.

Brass and oiled-wood furnishings gave the rail coach something of a nautical feel as well.

Local artist Webb Meredith worked eighteen to twenty hours a day for a week on the vehicle's exterior, painting scenes of St. Petersburg's beaches, waterfront and sporting activities and protecting it all with several coats of varnish.

While on tour, the Pullman was open to the general public for a walk-through tour and always a warm greeting from Sunshine Sam, the porter.

At the conclusion of each of their concerts, the Royal Scotch Highlanders handed out promotional flyers about St. Petersburg, took orders for their records and publicized their remaining schedule. Never before had any city undertaken such an ambitious "roving minstrel" approach to municipal publicity.

Martha Welch, wife of realty board president A.R. Welch, submitted the first of twenty-three entries suggesting the "Sunshine" name for the minstrel's coach, winning a twenty-five-dollar cash prize from the chamber of commerce on dedication day. Stebbins's daughter, Ruth, christened the brass-trimmed chariot with a bottle of orange juice in front of a crowd of nearly three thousand onlookers. Jim Coad, secretary-manager of the St. Petersburg Chamber of Commerce, told a Washington, D.C. realtor's convention later that year that the coach "had more than paid for itself" on its very first trip.

During its four-year run on the rails, the Sunshine Pullman traveled more than forty-five thousand miles, taking the Royal Scotch Highlanders into northern towns large and small; from Manitowoc, Wisconsin, to Washington, D.C. Local newspaper ads and feature stories about the band's arrival never failed to emphasize that the Highlanders were the "band that made St. Petersburg famous." In the summer of 1924 alone, the band performed

Known to his friends and passengers as "Sunshine Sam," the porter in charge of the city-owned Pullman stayed with the custom-designed coach when it was sold to the City of Miami.

350 concerts in twenty-one states before an estimated audience of 3 million people. During that one season, 10,000 visitors signed the guest log aboard the Sunshine Pullman and were added to the chamber's mailing list.

The Pullman deal was initially beneficial to all parties. Roy Smith's musicians, including the very popular tenor singer Bobbie Brollier, would perform an eight-week summer rail tour across northern and western states. Smith could book his own performances and negotiate ticket prices. The Highlanders could also sell their records—recorded, appropriately, on the Sunshine label. In exchange, the band handed out literally tons of flyers and booklets promoting St. Petersburg and hosted VIP tours of the railcar.

"We were surprised at how many people, who had previously been to Florida, wanted to see a pelican," said band director Smith. "We needed to add one—a stuffed one—to our traveling exhibit." The band was also obligated to perform a regular schedule of local afternoon and evening concerts free of charge in Williams Park during the peak tourist season. During nontouring periods, the Sunshine Pullman was used to transport

Rotary Club delegates and realty board members to their respective national conventions.

After a successful fourth season, squabbles over the $45,000 annual contract with the city apparently got in the way, and in 1927, Smith took his ensemble south to their new home in Miami. The Sunshine Pullman sat idle in the Seaboard Rail Yard for about nine months until the St. Petersburg Chamber finally agreed to sell it to the City of Miami for $5,000. The railcar was repainted and became known as the Spirit of Miami. But after only one season, a rift with the musician's union stopped the innovative bandwagon on its tracks and put an end to the Scotch Highlanders' far and wide travels.

Foley's Ferry

Before the Gandy Bridge, travel from St. Petersburg to Bradenton required a ninety-mile adventure. This trip followed a route through northern Pinellas, eastward to Tampa and then the final sixty-mile southwest stretch to Manatee County. Clearly, folks in southern Pinellas felt this to be an unnecessarily long trek for a destination only seven miles to the south.

Rather than using costly steel and concrete to span the mouth of Tampa Bay, St. Petersburg real estate pioneer J.G. Foley and civic booster Charles Carter decided on a more affordable solution: shuttle automobiles and their passengers across the bay by boat.

The partnership organized and launched the Bee Line Ferry Company in February 1926. The ferry departed from downtown St. Petersburg every forty-five minutes, heading south and docking at the northern tip of Manatee County.

The Bee Line's southern terminus, Piney Point, was reached in less than forty minutes, and traversed, as the company promoted, "the last American Frontier." The Bee Line was so popular it rapidly expanded to a fleet of three diesel ferryboats: the *Pinellas*, the *Manatee* and the *Sarasota*. Each day, the aptly named trio shuttled about 1,500 automobiles and their passengers—saving their clients forty-nine miles of non-air-conditioned driving each way.

A round trip cost three dollars, and passengers on foot or bicycle paid twenty-five cents each way. Due to a 2,000 percent increase in automobile traffic on Pinellas roads, the wait often took hours.

Nevertheless, the ride offered foodstuffs, as much salt air as one could breathe and a welcome respite from the bone-jarring drive around Tampa

Throughout the middle of the century, Triple A, the American Automobile Association, became one of the most respected travel authorities, insuring, assisting and informing travelers. Its endorsement was a valuable advertising and promotion tool.

Bay. "The value of this ferry can hardly be overestimated," claimed a 1926 *Tourist News* editorial. "St. Petersburg will be on direct route to Miami and other points in the extreme southern part of the state."

By the summer of 1927, tourism to Florida and St. Petersburg was again on the rise. Ernest Smith, president of the St. Petersburg Motor Club said he had received reports from the national headquarters of the American Automobile Association in Washington, D.C., which were "very positive." According to their statistics, slightly more than 113,000 automobiles crossed the state line near Jacksonville during the first five months of the year, compared to only 65,000 the previous year. Smith said his club had twice run out of maps, brochures and informational leaflets about St. Petersburg.

"The motorist movement is definitely on, and we must prepare for heavy traffic," he told city leaders. The motor club promoter said reprints of the Sunshine City tour guide would be distributed to more than seven hundred AAA clubs nationwide as quickly as possible.

At the same time, Miami city officials announced they had awarded a $42,000 contract to a St. Augustine printer for production of three promotional publications: a directory of hotels and apartments, a guide to tourist-agency services and a thirty-two-page booklet on the history and features of the South Florida mecca. Calling it the largest such contract in state history, more than 600,000 promotional pieces were produced.

Competition within the state for tourist dollars was becoming serious business. The library and advertising board of St. Petersburg didn't have the huge budget that Miami seemed to enjoy, but they proved to be up to the challenge of attracting tourists through an affordable publications program. And in a hugely popular decision, the St. Petersburg ad board kept its printing business local, awarding the contract to the Tourist News Publishing Company. Coming in almost $700 under its budget, three new printed pieces promoting the Sunshine City were produced. The main brochure was a twenty-four-page, four-color general tourist/resident information booklet; 150,000 copies were produced. The remaining two pieces included an apartment directory and a smaller guide to sporting activities. With a total budget of $15,000, ad committee chairman Robert Walden said quality and price were prime considerations but supporting local business was equally important.

Busboys to Businessmen

Many events coalesced in St. Petersburg in the early 1920s to create the whirlwind real estate rush known, primarily after its collapse in 1925–26, as the boom years. Whether it was Henry Ford's suggestion of a five-dollar-a-day minimum wage combined with massive postwar layoffs or the 1921 Gulf Coast hurricane, which prompted massive repairs and construction in Pinellas, that sent investors southbound with pockets full of life savings and severance pay is unclear.

What is certain, however, is that for several untamed years, St. Petersburg, like many Florida communities, rapidly expanded. Scores of impressive hotels and hundreds of apartment units sprang up from the once-barren sandlots throughout the Sunshine City. The resulting building frenzy fed the dreams of many men bent on spanning the bays surrounding Pinellas.

Between the construction of the Gandy Bridge and the Bee Line Ferry, Florida's latest building bubble began to deteriorate. Speculation and greed made way for railroad embargoes on the East Coast, prompting the wrath of northern bankers. With the capsizing of the *Prinz Valdemar* in Miami Harbor in January 1925 and the jammed shipping routes that followed, little else could damage the speculative mood of Florida, or so many thought.

Paper profits were like confetti blown to the wind by September 1926, when a mighty hurricane blew through Miami, pushing Florida into an economic tailspin years ahead of the rest of the nation.

Within a few weeks following the Bee Line's inaugural run, John Lodwick and other city representatives, along with railroad officials, chamber members, bankers and merchants statewide, gathered in Jacksonville. Chaired by Peter O. Knight, the "Florida Takes Inventory Congress" sought to address the concerns of civic leaders from dozens of communities in response to the sudden shift in prosperous times.

Nearly as quick as the building boom made businessmen out of busboys, it had come to a screeching halt. In several short years, St. Petersburg had more infrastructures and vacant lots than it could fill in several decades. Massive road-paving projects, sewer and water distribution points and platted subdivisions lay idle.

While significant improvements and advancements had been achieved by St. Petersburg during the boom years, the majority of land now stood vacant as unfulfilled visions. Consider that in the November 22, 1925 edition of the *St. Petersburg Times*, there were over 130 pages advertising such sales alone.

"But, remember, the 1925 boom was not an urge to retire to a pleasant cottage in Florida or bask in luxurious villas or seaside hotels," wrote realtor cum historian Walter P. Fuller of the frenzy. "It was, instead, a greedy delirium to acquire riches overnight without benefit of effort, brains, or services rendered."

It would seem that few could compete with the bust and its impact on tourism in Florida. Fortunately for St. Petersburg, the city had its sunshine, superlative surroundings and miles of new roads, along with instrumental bridges and ferries connecting the city to points east, west and south. Because it still housed unlimited boosters and boasters eager to sell St. Petersburg to the tourist trade, the city fared better than most during those dark days. More importantly, however, the Sunshine City employed a most sophisticated weapon during those cloudy days: the master of media attention John Lodwick.

Chapter Two

THE CITY THAT ADVERTISING BUILT

Although it had taken John Lodwick less than ten minutes to pitch his promotional services to St. Petersburg Board of Trade secretary L.A. Whitney, he spent the rest of his life selling the Sunshine City. Hired on the spot in 1918, Lodwick had made his way to St. Petersburg with the intention of becoming the first press agent for a Florida city.

In those early days, few knew of St. Petersburg's charm and endless sunshine, and even fewer knew of the ample sunbathing and sporting events available on its shores. During his nearly two-decade tenure, noted a 1938 *Evening Independent* editorial, John Lodwick's "constant pounding of the name St. Petersburg made it one of the world's best known resorts."

Lodwick's method was as ingenious as it was cost-effective. At a time when Jack Frost was tweaking northern noses, his pictures of bathing beauties frolicking in one-piece swimsuits and beckoning to visit the Sunshine City garnered national press.

All industry-free St. Petersburg had to sell was its sunshine, sand and inviting environment. With the clever and cunning John Lodwick on the scene, St. Petersburg rapidly rose to world championship status—literally. Starting as the mid-1920s land boom was withering, Lodwick devised a plan to make St. Petersburg the headquarters for myriad sports competitions.

Tossing a tag line of "World Championship" on activities such as shuffleboard, horseshoes, chess and lawn bowling, the city appeared in sports and society pages in newspapers from Reno to Roanoke.

John Lodwick never tired of looking for different ways to lure folks to St. Petersburg. *Personal Collection of Rui Farias*

So well known was Lodwick's influence as the man who organized National Horseshoe Championships that his rules and regulations of the "game every boy in America can get into" appeared in publications nationally.

Like many masters of semantic sculpting, John Lodwick engaged his audience at a personal level. Publicity material and other professional promotional prose recognized the consumer's penchant for activity and adventure, as well as their desire for being seen in the "playground of [one's] dream," whether they stayed for a weekend or a winter season. Advertisements appearing in the January 1923 *New York Times*, for example, reminded readers they could travel to St. Petersburg, "where the sunshine is in people's hearts as well overhead," in a mere forty-four hours.

"An alluring city for rest or relaxation," 1920s St. Petersburg offered "golfing, bathing, boating, fishing, trap-shooting, tennis," and "comfortable seats everywhere to rest and enjoy the sunshine and pastimes."

In 1922, St. Petersburg physician E.J. Melville published the first of several articles on the benefits of Florida weather, claiming it would cure everything from asthma to rickets. His essay "The Curative Value of Florida Sunshine," published in the *International Journal of Surgery*, promotes heliotherapy, a fancy term for nude sunbathing: "All that is required is that the patient spend most of the day lying naked in the sun with the eyes shaded from the glare." The medical journal article was subsequently quoted in a dozen or so national publications. Like decades of earlier tales and teatime stories of

Roque competitors concentrating on the perfect spin pitch in one of the many recreational activities John Lodwick promoted as a World Championship Event. The sport was a one-time-only summer Olympics game in 1904 with only the United States competing.

Florida being home to the fabled Fountain of Youth, the healthy sunshine "prescription" attracted tourists to the boxes and the beaches. One theory proposed the health benefit was due in large part to the city's geographic location; longitude 27 degrees, 42 minutes, when traced around the globe was purported to be the best angle at which to absorb the sun's healing properties. Science has made progress since then.

Solaria popularity prospered for about two decades. The City of St. Petersburg built and operated the Municipal Solarium, which opened on February 1, 1930, and was equipped with private stalls, wooden slat chaise lounges and towel service. Facilities for men and women were separated by a fifteen-foot-high wall. During its five-month inaugural season, which closed the last day of June 1949, people had patronized the tanning facility. In addition to the city-owned center, the Princess Martha and Vinoy were among several hotels to promote and offer rooftop sun bathing to their guests.

With the Million Dollar Pier as a backdrop, a trio of skiers is all smiles in this city publicity postcard mailed worldwide. Some six decades later, an exhibit on the city's pier history included this same free-spirited image. A smiling museum guest pointed at the girl in the black suit and proclaimed, "That's me from another life! We had such a good time doing those publicity shots."

Some entrepreneurs sold sunshine by the hour, complete with nurse and maid services, packaged in unique turntable booths like those at the St. Petersburg Solaria.

Known as Brewer Rotary Wooden Cabinets, the tanning booths were designed and built by A.D. Brewer, a local carpenter and backyard inventor.

His precut kits were sold by local lumber companies. Until early 2013, a full-size version of his tanning booth was nestled among the palms and greenery on the grounds of the Vinoy Hotel, visible from Beach Drive.

With no hesitation, St. Petersburg sold itself as "the playground of your dreams, with accommodations to suit everyone." Indeed, the chamber of commerce suggested, the city was a virtual paradise for all who entered.

Attempting to distinguish between the "staged" and the "authentic" vacation may have been less of a concern in early twentieth-century promotional

Sparkling water, wispy clouds in a sun-filled sky, a pretty girl in a bathing suit tempting a pelican with a treat—what travel editor wouldn't want to publish this shot? *Photo courtesy Jack Swenningsen.*

Posing guests in front of a painted backdrop, complete with palm tree and a biwing airboat light, was a quick way for John Lodwick's photographers to get plenty of photos to send to hometown newspaper editors.

literature, suggest authors Hans Christian Anderson and Mike Robinson while investigating the consequences of literature on tourism.

While literature's relationship with tourism may indeed be little more than a "created cultural form," as Anderson and Robinson propose, for Lodwick the distinction muddled inspiration and interaction for St. Petersburg–bound tourists who sought the city of sunshine for adventure and activity.

Known for his aptly titled "Lodwick Technique," the pitchman gathered newly registered guests and took their photos alongside a recent catch from the pier, beside a bathing beauty or under a shady palm tree. Anything indicative of the grand time tourists could have was fair game for John Lodwick. After a little polish and creative editing, he would then submit the "candid" shot with a prewritten script to the travelers' hometown newspapers. With about 25 percent of all visitors registering with the chamber of commerce and society clubs and Lodwick's endless effort to make contact with each guest, St. Petersburg received untold dollars worth of publicity as hometown editors eagerly printed their citizens' exploits in the Sunshine City.

Those tourists who had their photos captured and captioned by Lodwick surely did not mind playing a lead role in the Florida fantasy. Moreover, for many readers, his promotional literature and accompanying photographs were viewed as creative art, both stylistically and emotionally engaging. The "reality" of John Lodwick's approach, however, mattered little since his imaginings often became genuine for the visiting tourist—or at least by the time their adventure was repeatedly retold back home.

Prescribing Paradise

Since the final days of the nineteenth century, the attributes of St. Petersburg received rave reviews and encouraging editorials, very much in the same manner that John Lodwick successfully emulated two decades later. One particular example attests to the unlimited advantage of the testimonial and the space afforded to the personal communiqué. Published in Woodstock, Virginia, the 1899 testament of Virginian J.L. Wisman appeared in the *Shenandoah Herald* on the following Valentine's Day:

> *ST. PETERSBURG, Fla.*
> *January 31, 1899*
>
> *Mr. Editor:—*
>
> *I would like to tell you something of this, my second visit to this beautiful town, and, first of all of the delightful weather in this the most favored section of Sunny Florida. It is seldom that one seeks a fire here, and so far as the temperature is concerned, it is all that one could wish.*
>
> *St. Petersburg's growth since I was here two years ago has been magical. Sixth avenue, the business street, and on which is located the Detroit and other hotels, has shelled streets, taken from deposits of fish bone shells, etc., found in the creeks and bayous, which make a beautiful and substantial roadway. It is a beautiful sight looking shoreward from the bay. A gradual rise of 60 feet to the half-mile brings out prominently every portion of the town, and the pier which runs out three-quarters of a mile to deep water, always presents some features of interest to the stranger.*
>
> *There is no doubt in my mind, having visited all sections of this state, but that St. Petersburg and vicinity enjoy many natural advantages not possessed by any other section of Florida.*
>
> *I actually believe if the people of Virginia and the more northern states had the slightest idea of conditions as they really exist in Florida, the state would not be large enough to entertain the guests to say nothing of those who would make this their future home. I have not found the "spring of perpetual youth," for which Ponce de Leon hunted so assiduously, but am thoroughly satisfied with my trip and know that I am greatly benefited.*
>
> *J.L. Wisman*

So enthralled was Wisman with St. Petersburg he continued to winter in the city for the next several years. Rarely missing an opportunity to share his knowledge of the growing city with the good folks of Woodstock, he regularly wrote to the *Shenandoah.*

Again, the power and persuasion of testimonials are apparent in a final look at the optimistic writings of J.L. Wisman:

> *ST. PETERSBURG, Fla.*
> *Feb. 5, 1902*
>
> *Mr. Editor:*
>
> *As my former letters to the HERALD have escaped the waste basket I will ask your kind indulgence once more, as this is the shortest means of communication to my friends in old Virginia. It reaches a larger circle than I could by letters…*

Wisman then closed his letter by listing more than seventy amenities that the Sunshine City enjoyed. He was far from alone in lauding the land of sunshine and selling St. Petersburg

As early as 1874, the medical profession sought a climate conducive to patient recovery and relaxation. They found it in Florida. In April 1885, at the New Orleans American Medical Association conference, Dr. Washington Chew Van Bibber spoke of the benefits of Gulf Coast climate and topography.

First suggested by London physician B.W. Richardson in 1874, the search for a "Health City" captivated many. Dr. Van Bibber answered the call in a summation of surveys and findings conducted by several field researchers. His conclusion declared Pinellas and its islands the healthiest and "best climate in Florida."

Entitled "Peninsular and Sub-Peninsular Air and Climates: A Contribution to Sanitary Science, relating especially to the climate and healthfulness of Pinellas Peninsula, Florida," Dr. Van Bibber's paper stressed several particulars. The first of them were scientific findings suggesting peninsulas and sub-peninsulas, such as Pinellas, benefited from advanced air and climate qualities more than their landlocked counterparts. Dr. Van Bibber's proposition to sanitarium science called for the immediate construction of a "Health City," and when completed, he affirmed, "invalids and pleasure seekers, from all lands, will come to enjoy the delights of a winter climate, which, all things considered can probably have no equal elsewhere."

In answering the question of where to build such a city, Van Bibber's paper unequivocally stated construction of such a community would prosper on the Pinellas Peninsula, adjacent to the "Gulf of Mexico, with the broad waters of a beautiful bay nearly surrounding it."

By 1914, additional tempting testimonials found their way into the February edition of *Florida's Health Notes*. Published monthly by Florida's State Board of Health, the publication listed the vital statistics of various cities.

One particular report by city health officer Dr. William M. Davis investigates St. Petersburg's mortality rates. Dr. Davis summarized that "the low resident death rates corroborates what St. Petersburg claims to be—a health resort." While early publicity of Pinellas owes much to these medical testimonials, one must note here the interest of two other men, Gustave Gehring and Frank A. Davis, who heard of Van Bibber's high praise for the Pinellas area and its seemingly therapeutic environs.

In 1892, seven years after Dr. Van Bibber's proposal, local settler Zephaniah Phillips sold forty-five acres of his Long Key, Florida homestead to Dr. Gustave P. Gehring, who proposed building a sanitarium on the barrier key. However, his dream of an island oasis for the infirm, which had cost him $800, died in less than three years. By 1895, Dr. Gehring sold his shares, at a $200 profit, to four enterprising souls who attempted to create their own enclave, Morey Beach, named after the principal investor.

Phillips, Long Key's first homesteader, held the deed to an additional thirty-five acres and platted his land under a more familiar name, Pass-a-Grille City.

Additional attempts to alter portions of Pinellas into a themed landscape continued. In 1906, Frank A. Davis, with the backing of Captain J.F. Chase, purchased two hundred acres of nearby Disston City (modern-day Gulfport), intending to create a Civil War veterans' hideaway and retirement paradise. Like Florida's largest landowner Hamilton Disston before him, F.A Davis bragged of southern Pinellas but faced lackluster results in selling his tropical oasis.

Throughout the later part of the century, Davis, who had been in New Orleans when Van Bibber read his "Health City" paper, utilized his Philadelphia publishing company to reprint the report many times over. According to Robert Craven Jr., grandnephew to F.A. Davis, his great-uncle was greatly influenced by Van Bibber's 1885 AMA conference report. For several years, Davis printed promotional pamphlets about the Pinellas Peninsula and its salutary benefits.

From his "Facts and Suggestions for Persons Forced to Seek Permanent or Temporary Homes on the Pinellas Peninsula," compiled in 1896, and his 1901 "Progress and Possibilities of St. Petersburg," to his 1906 "Souvenir—St. Petersburg, the Pleasure City of the South," F.A. Davis encouraged northern doctors and tourists to experience Florida's healthiest spot.

Several years later, with the Disston/Veteran City debacle behind him and requiring the healthy climes of Florida himself, Frank A. Davis proposed building a sanitarium in nearby Tarpon Springs.

Again, the idea failed due to lack of interest. Nevertheless, the city of St. Petersburg benefited greatly. By 1924, as the Gandy Bridge was nearing completion, Davis brought an electrical plant to St. Petersburg and many other infrastructures required of a growing city.

Although he was not a direct owner, Van Bibber, in the 1850s, sent his son Claude and three investing Baltimoreans to secure what he deemed the best portion of Pinellas. Their purchase of the Pinellas Point from Maximo Hernandez's widow, the area's first homesteaders, never saw the first sign of development and foreclosed. The investment group quietly abandoned the land for back taxes.

Though it may have been Dr. Van Bibber's financial goal to promote the area, it was certainly the countless references by Frank A. Davis and subsequent reprinting of the Van Bibber report that secured Pinellas's attraction to northern visitors and encouraged doctors in prescribing the destination for consumptives and invalids.

"We can thank Providence for the peninsular setting, the blue skies, waters and sunshine," reported the *Times* a century later. "It just needed a little promotion. For that we can thank the physician who proclaimed St. Petersburg the healthiest spot on Earth."

Liquid to Land

After years of publicity stunts and promotions, St. Petersburg's entrance into the second decade of the twentieth century was unmistakable. The Sunshine City soon outpaced nearly every Florida town in growth and construction. Rivaling Miami Beach, while surpassing Jacksonville and Tampa across the bay, St. Petersburg recorded well over $20 million worth of building in 1925 alone. Accompanying the bay bridges and ferry service, extensive changes occurred on Tampa Bay's waterfront.

Turning liquid into land, as the adage goes, developers trenched and filled along the shorelines, creating artificial inlets and man-made islands for further speculation and lot sales. Resident C. Perry Snell epitomized the phrase "land developer" through his dredged enclave, Snell Isle.

Many of the landscapes featured in the latter 1920s advertisements simply were not there a few years prior. While much annexed land had come into St. Petersburg's tax rolls, additional land literally came forth from the oceans. During the heady boom years (1921–26), St. Petersburg proper expanded from eleven acres to fifty-three acres in size. Drastic alterations of the land occurred as developers emulated Tampa's Davis Islands and Carl Fisher's Miami Beach by scouring the bottoms of bays for salvageable sand to dredge and build on.

Where once stood a small spoil island, often submerged at high tide, land appeared nearly overnight. C. Perry Snell, self-proclaimed pioneer land developer and donator of downtown waterfront parks, opened the upscale Snell Isle subdivision in late 1925. His promotional plan called for clubhouses, golf courses and fine, stately homes, all on a pristine, yet pricey 275-acre island.

Actually, Snell probably had less than forty or fifty acres that were above sea level at the time; but then came the dredges, dikes and determined men and machines that transformed St. Petersburg's bays and waterfronts.

Some beach locations included decks and diving platforms for the more adventurous; many preferred to just wade in the relaxing waters of Tampa Bay.

Tourists-turned-buyers had their choices of hotels to pass the time during construction; however, Snell shrewdly offered accommodations, built on site, and recreation while they waited. From shuffleboard and sunbathing to unexcelled golf and gulf fishing, tourists had endless options in St. Petersburg. There were concerts in Williams Park, horseshoes and lawn bowling on just about every open public park and, for those wishing to move their card games or nightly dancing closer to the water's edge, the newly created Million Dollar Pier.

Since 1889, a pier of some fashion has extended from St. Petersburg's shores, stretching thousands of feet into Tampa Bay. The railroad pier, over a half mile in length, offered unlimited opportunities for anglers, sunbathers and the carefree who dared the pier's toboggan slide. Following years of pier wars, waterfront improvement initiatives and the devastating 1921 hurricane, boosters and civic leaders pushed for a grander replacement to the beloved attraction.

With a name to match the construction costs, the Million Dollar Pier opened in 1926 to immediate fanfare. The Mediterranean-themed pier, thought by many to be *Independent* publisher Lew Brown's brainchild, offered dancing, shopping and recreation. The 1926 incarnation added an "instant destination for sun-seeking tourists to visit—and spend their money in St. Petersburg," reminisced the *St. Petersburg Times* some seven decades later.

An aerial view of the Million Dollar Pier surrounded by hundreds of automobiles and tourists. Spa Beach and the opulent Vinoy Hotel can be seen in the background.

As city boundaries expanded and scores of impressive boomtime hotels soared skyward, so did land prices and census figures. St. Petersburg's citizen count, which topped fourteen thousand by 1920, had nearly doubled as the boom was in full swing four years later. It paled in comparison, however, to the tens of thousands of annual visitors to the area. If automobile traffic figures offer indications of St. Petersburg's success, then consider that in the first eighteen months since the 1924 opening of the Gandy Bridge, more than one million vehicles carrying Floridians, tourists and their cargo crossed Tampa Bay.

Blessed with large and lavish hotels and more than seven thousand rooms for rent, 1920s St. Petersburg had truly become a major tourist destination. Travelers who dared not part with their hard-earned pay yet yearned to see the southernmost state flocked to Florida in their Model T Fords.

Ford's Freeloaders

Lodging in Florida underwent drastic changes as the automobile invaded the tourist scene. While hotels remained the preferred choice for many guests, automobile enthusiasts embraced the freedoms that auto-camping brought, both financially and figuratively. In less than three decades, Henry Ford's Model T dominated the motorist movement. Lovingly labeled the Tin Lizzie, more than 15 million Model Ts rolled off Detroit, Michigan assembly lines.

Straining its thin, twelve-spoke wheels and twenty-horsepower engine, determined drivers destined for a Florida retreat outfitted their touring cars with almost anything needed for the journey. Packed with overflowing provisions, many of which were in tin cans, automobiles of all makes came together on the shores of Florida. Henry Ford himself became a regular sight in the Sunshine State.

"I will build a motor car for the great multitude," Henry Ford believed, "constructed of the best materials, by the best men to be hired, after the simplest designs that modern engineering can devise." More importantly and instrumental, Ford added, his motor car would be "so low in price that no man making a good salary will be unable to own one and enjoy with his family the blessings of hours of pleasure in God's great open spaces."

Living up to his own message, Henry Ford spent countless moments touring and examining "God's great open spaces" in his Model T, cruising on tires his passenger Harvey Firestone manufactured. In a car he built,

Ford often went camping with such luminaries as Thomas Edison, Teddy Roosevelt and Warren Harding. Both Edison and Ford found Florida's west coast climate ideal.

By 1916, after two decades of friendship, Ford and Edison became Floridian neighbors in nearby Fort Myers just south of St. Petersburg.

Henry Ford's tourist advice and touring automobiles transformed many southern cities. The boom in auto-camping led to the creation of public campgrounds in tourism-dependent cities around the bay. In St. Petersburg and Tampa, the tin can tourist was a welcomed sight—at first.

"Practically every Florida town and city, large and small, located inland or on the gulf," described an early travelogue, "provides a tin can town or tin can village for the tin can tourist."

Under the direction of Mayor Noel Mitchell, St. Petersburg's public Tent City provided low-cost, short-term accommodations to the independent, automobile-based traveler. Intended to attract visitors who could not—or would not—spend their hard-earned dollars on hotel fees, many Florida cities hoped that automobile and trailer parks would recoup these losses in amenities and service fees. The success of the 1920–21 tin can tourist season was soon overshadowed by growing resentment toward "freeloaders."

Many tin can towns found "that an open handed and unsupervised welcome to any person…will bring nothing but annoyances, losses, and misery." Considered pariahs endeavoring to live on the cheap and undercutting seasonal labor wages, summarized one historian, it was unsurprising that many citizens discourage the invasion of "automobile hobos." When the expected economic windfall failed to appear, many parks closed or turned to privatization. Such was the case for St. Petersburg's public Tent City.

While criticism followed Noel Mitchell's campground initiative, few complained about his greatest contribution to the Sunshine City and its everlasting promotion: the grand and plentiful downtown benches.

Originally constructed in 1907, with broad seats, high backs and painted orange, Mayor Mitchell's addition of wooden benches outside his downtown St. Petersburg real estate business caught the attention of weary tourists and local merchants. Designed to offer plenty of room for the fatigued soul and space for Noel "the Sandman" Mitchell's advertisements, business storefronts soon sprouted their own comfort stations.

Several years, and mayoral elections later, the lack of uniform sizes, color and garish advertisements prompted Mayor Al Lang to set a few standards. First, the benches must all match in dimensions, Lang insisted. More

The green benches were the daily place to see and be seen, but eventually, they came to represent what was thought to be an old-folks'-home image.

importantly, all benches were to be the same color. The mayor mandated a deep, dark green as the sole color.

Amid grumbling and protest, the ordinance took effect in 1916, creating an instant trademark for the city of St. Petersburg. In the decades to follow Mitchell's construction, and Lang's subsequent standardization of the beloved benches, several thousand people in all paid homage to St. Petersburg's dedication to recuperation, relaxation and recreation.

Sunshine and Suckers

By 1924, advertisements in the *New York Times* claimed an estimated fifty thousand sightseers annually visited St. Petersburg, making it "one of Florida's most beautiful and popular winter resorts." Many tourists and land speculators choose to hang about and make their homes in the Sunshine City. The larger the geographically southern municipality of St. Petersburg grew, however, the more "northern" in citizenry it became.

With each passing census, the city housed more and more New England and American heartland residents, eager to escape the brutal cold seasons. John Lodwick's widely submitted articles enticed the freezing citizens of

North America with promises of idle days in store for "winter visitors who have sought out this haven of relief from the colds and chills" that were prevalent in northern climes. Historians Stockbridge and Perry point out that St. Petersburg followed the trend of many other southern cities by adopting the nickname of Sunshine City.

Marketing on that theme, as early as 1910, St. Petersburg's *Evening Independent* newspaper gave away, free of charge, every copy that came off the presses any day the sun failed to appear.

Lew Brown, the *Independent*'s editor and vigorous promoter of St. Petersburg's public waterfront, called his faith in the dear old sol's penchant for gracing Pinellas with its health rays the "Sunshine Offer."

Recalling P.T. Barnum's famous quip "that any man who should connect his advertising with the weather would make a tenstrike," Lew Brown rolled out his "Sunshine Offer" in September 1910 with a full-page announcement. Word of the offer soon spread nationwide. "After two or three years," reminisced Brown decades later, "full-page illustrated write-ups of the

A patriotic "newsie" delivery boy proudly sports a navy cap, possibly that of a brother or his father. Look closely at the front fender for the image of Uncle Sam pointing an "I want you" finger.

Sunshine offer were printed in the [multi]colored Sunday supplements of practically all the great daily newspapers of the United States, giving it fourteen million [in] circulation."

Well into modern times, the *Independent* continued the tradition of free newspapers on sunless days, averaging no more than a half dozen editions per year.

From the unwavering promotions and boasting from civic boosters like Frank Davis, Lew Brown and John Lodwick, St. Petersburg's catchphrase, "the Sunshine City," could have very easily been "the City that Advertising Built," as Stockbridge and Perry suggested in 1926. "For there is no other community in all Florida," the authors note in *Florida in the Making*, "in which the united efforts of the entire citizenship have been so acutely and intelligently concentrated upon advertising its advantages."

For all the hullabaloo and high praises of St. Petersburg and Florida's west coast, the Roaring Twenties seemed an unstoppable era of wealth and growth. Realtors and binder-boys hawking the latest subdivision plan or available plat of land dominated the St. Petersburg scene. So tempting was the rags-to-riches delusion in St. Petersburg that the city claimed over six thousand realtors residing within its borders during the boom.

Housing prices soared as investors and schemers sought out the Sunshine City for a quick profit. The roar was quick to turn into a whimper, however, following the local real estate crash of the mid-1920s. Buyers-turned-believers of the Florida Dream drove prices to the brink. Walter Fuller, once one of the largest landowners and developers of Pinellas County, summarized the frenzy as "one of the periodic epidemics of gambling that have swept this country…a something-for-nothing fever with more color and substance than most."

December 7, 1925—sixteen years before and an ocean away from the attack on Pearl Harbor—was a day that indeed would live in infamy for many locals and investors as the clouds and skies over St. Petersburg grew more ominous and imminent with each passing hour.

As 1926 was approaching, the tourist season was at its pinnacle. On this very same day, delegates throughout the nation gathered in the city for a weeklong convention of the Investment Bankers Association. Greeted with endless rain and chilly winds, the Sunshine City and its guests had cold and wet days ahead. The uninviting weather lasted the whole convention.

Convinced that claims of St. Petersburg's endless sunshine were little more than boom-era ballyhoo, visiting bankers and financial investors left disgruntled and doubtful that the Florida boom should or could continue. Investment bankers and city representatives hailing from other states encouraged citizens to be wary of Florida investments. Some even forewarned the bust.

Declaring to the *Wall Street Journal* that if Florida cities continued overextending themselves financially based on speculation and city indebtedness, one investor insisted, "a bad condition is going to come about and the credit of Florida [will] be impaired."

Suddenly, the land boom ended as unexpectedly as it had begun. "The 1925 Florida land boom just ran out of fuel in the late fall of 1925 and quit—we just ran out of suckers. That's all. We got all their money," quipped historian Walter Fuller.

"Did I say that we ran out of suckers?" No, that wasn't quite correct, Fuller mused decades later, "*We* became the suckers."

Inflating a Grounded Economy

Between 1926 and 1927, St. Petersburg's construction and land speculation all but disappeared. Gone were the multitudes of laborers, construction crews, realtors and the vast personnel support system required of a booming metropolis. Although a minor exodus occurred during these years, the tourist trade, which the city had manifested since its inception, continued as northern investors and visitors rode Wall Street to the dizzying heights experienced prior to the nationwide economic downturn.

Not all construction halted after the local speculation bust. Through civic cajoling and government intervention, St. Petersburg's declaration of an industry-free waterfront created much dredging activity a few miles southward, in the Bayboro Harbor.

Constructed as a base of operation against Prohibition-incited rumrunners and bootleggers, the U.S. Coast Guard opened a station on landfill created by the recent widening of shipping lanes. Additional acreage of Bayboro fill—dredged, dumped and molded into land—turned into tarmacs, hangers and airplanes. By 1929, Albert Whitted Airport opened for commercial aviation.

Seizing this golden opportunity, city publicity director Lodwick called for an additional use of the aviation facility prior to its completion. In response to the grounded 1928 economy, he staged a soaring publicity stunt.

Press releases announced the newest coming attraction to St. Petersburg: a Goodyear Blimp. Through his close and personal ties with businessmen

A Goodyear blimp ground crew steadies the aircraft's passenger gondola while three female passengers appear to be admiring the dashing dirigible pilot.

and editors around the nation, Lodwick secured a small dirigible for the Sunshine City. Nearly half a football field in length and thirty-seven feet in circumference, the Goodyear-Zeppelin Corporation's *Puritan* hailed from Lodwick's home state of Ohio. The Akron-based airship selected St. Petersburg as its southern base of operations, intending to study the area's climate and potential for future passenger possibilities.

Key West Citizen subscribers read John Lodwick's prediction that the arrival of the *Puritan* would be the first of its kind in Florida, and "when the famous craft makes its initial appearance," he boasted, "100,000 west Floridians and winter visitors" will gather at Albert Whitted Airport to watch history in the making. Furthermore, Lodwick claimed, "It is said that most of Florida travel from the North within the next ten years will be by this type of aircraft."

Little did Lodwick know that uncertainty would soon strike Wall Street or that Eastern Air Transport would extend its flying operations from New York into St. Petersburg. Both events aided in labeling Lodwick's ambitions a "flying folly."

The Goodyear *Puritan* floats over the St. Petersburg waterfront toward the Vinoy Hotel.

"Even John Lodwick, the master of the well-timed publicity stunt, had not foreseen the stock market crash of October 1929," historian Raymond Arsenault said of the city's flying white elephant and costly storage. "As the hanger went up, the values of stock went down. And as the blimp glided among the clouds, the lofty dreams of the Sunshine City came crashing down."

Between 1930 and 1931, as every bank went insolvent, the speculative spending and extensive use of bonds for improvements saddled St. Petersburg with the nation's second-highest indebtedness of over $800 per capita. Left with a huge overdue bill from an excessive past, like nearly every other city government, St. Petersburg was ill equipped for the difficulties brought on by the Great Depression. At the same time that the national economy shrank by $15 billion, Florida tourism drastically decreased. By April 1930, real estate sales and total value of building permits plummeted to an all-time low.

The worst was yet to come.

At a staggering $24 million, 1925 building permit values made investors giddy. However, 1932's total value of building permits exceeded barely $250,000.

Undeniably, St. Petersburg's boom-fueled growth had ended, displacing more than ten thousand residents. Forty thousand residents remained in St. Petersburg to weather out the storm ahead.

When the economy turned sour, St. Petersburg's famous, friendly green benches were a very lonely place for the down and out.

In addition to recognizing tourists from all the visiting states, the Festival of States parades provided local commerce an opportunity to promote their names. In 1938, this anniversary float featured Uncle Sam and dozens of current and past queen and princess honorees.

During his first forty-eight hours in office, President Franklin D. Roosevelt ordered all banks closed for a four-day national "banking holiday," priming the pump for his "New Deal" campaign platform. Within months, Roosevelt's "alphabet agencies" such as the Civilian Works Administration (CWA), the Works Progress Administration (WPA) and the Public Works Administration (PWA) came to dominate the thoughts of congressmen and citizens across the United States.

Locally in St. Petersburg, officials and civic leaders formulated long-range plans, ensuring brighter days for the Depression-laden Sunshine City. Times were hard across the nation, but "at no time during the depression did St. Petersburg have an unemployment problem as acute as that of hundreds of industrial cities throughout the nation," wrote Tampa Bay historian Karl Grismer. With the masterminding of publicity prince John Lodwick and his tireless staff, the chamber of commerce continued as the catalyst that kept St. Petersburg pushing forward in times of feast and in famine. Major relief, to those remaining craftsmen and laborers eager to earn, came to St. Petersburg early in the Depression.

The Great American Monopoly

Whether it was indeed the recuperating benefits of Pinellas and the offer of free waterfront property by city boosters or simply government foresightedness matters little compared to the boosts in budgets and morale that followed the building of a local veterans' hospital. Employing about one thousand workers, over $3 million flowed into the local economy as the nearly eight-hundred-acre Bay Pines tract changed from wild thickets of mangroves, palms and pines into the Southeast's primary Veterans' Administration Hospital and regional headquarters.

The VA hospital project was coupled with a pledge to also allocate a part of the PWA's $15 million budget to strengthen the U.S. Coast Guard.

Almost $700,000 went toward the Bayboro Harbor as massive construction resulted in seaplane hangars and air bases.

While National Airlines began its operations from St. Petersburg's Albert Whitted Airfield, offering round trips to Daytona Beach and back, civic boosting urged tourists to continue their travel plans, "get a Sunshine Perspective" and "Come on Down to the Sunny Side of Life" in the Sunshine City. "What America needs is a sunny outlook on life, and the logical place to get it," insisted the chamber of commerce, "is on the West Coast of Florida—at Sunny St. Petersburg."

Furthermore, newspaper advertisements acknowledged the drastic decrease in tourism and instructed readers to "follow the crowds southward...give yourself a rare vacation in the Sunshine City. Thousand are already here—and more are on the way." Tourism figures had shrunken to such low figures during the Depression that Roger Babson, a well-reputed statistician, urged Florida cities and civic leaders "to seek fame as a health center." Speaking to Tampa Bay advertisers and Kiwanis, Babson stated, "Florida has only one American monopoly—sunshine and climate." Capitalize on those two Florida constants and America's nearly 15 million folks over the age of sixty, suggested Babson, and Florida will rebound.

St. Petersburg was well ahead of Babson's prediction and recorded tourism figures that had not been equaled since 1928, totaling over thirty-one thousand registered visitors during the 1932–33 season. However, average tourist spending was considerably less than previous years.

Babson and the chamber of commerce were not alone in the promotion of paradise. During the first several years of the Great Depression, John Lodwick's endless editorials and articles selling the Sunshine City, its Festival of States parade and the St. Petersburg–Havana boat races blanketed the nation. From the likes of the *Chicago Daily Tribune* and the *Charleston Gazette* to the *Kingston Daily Freeman* and the *Indiana Evening Gazette*, John Lodwick touted St. Petersburg's ability to look past hard times and focus on fun and pleasurable events for tourists of every lifestyle.

At some point in the mid-1930s, wrote city historian Karl Grismer, the sense of hopelessness and dread eased throughout the nation. Locally, recovery from the Great Depression, "largely due to the indomitable spirit of St. Petersburg's citizens," came earlier than for most. During the worst of times, "instead of weeping and wailing, they kept planning for the future"; they supported the chamber of commerce, insisting that tourist advertising continue.

Reports soon circulated claiming the post-holiday influx of winter visitors in 1934 was the largest in the history of the Sunshine City. Less than two months following the devastating Labor Day hurricane of 1935 that lashed through southern Florida, chamber ads and John Lodwick, mentioning nothing of the storm, focused on the area's endless sunshine. Even the mayor, prompted by the "See Florida First" program, began listing the advantages of St. Petersburg, which had attracted visitors from all states of the Union, every province in Canada and twenty-six other foreign countries.

"St. Petersburg is devoted almost entirely to the exclusive entertainment of the traveling public," said Mayor John S. Smith. Predicting an onslaught of visitors well near the half million mark, Mayor Smith proclaimed that not only do tourists feel the Sunshine City is like a second home, but also with each passing year, "St. Petersburg's winter population assumes greater proportion."

Even in the midst of the national recession and an uncertain future, citizens urged boosters to spend more on promotions.

The chamber of commerce and John Lodwick responded to citizens' cries, insisting on continued northern advertising, with catchy jingles.

Promotions of the mid-1930s spoke of St. Petersburg's "amazing variety of recreation and entertainment…literally something to do, to see and enjoy every happy hour" and sold St. Petersburg as the "perfect place to wait out the depression."

No worries exist in the city, "Happy Days Are Here Again," claimed advertisements. "Why endure the discomforts of cold weather when it is so easy to come to sunny St. Petersburg?" asked the chamber.

"Pick up and pack up—leave cold and care behind—and hit the trail for the land of palms and flowers and the city of Sunshine," another ad prompted. And St. Petersburg's sunshine was exactly what city publicity director Lodwick had been keenly watching for the last year and half.

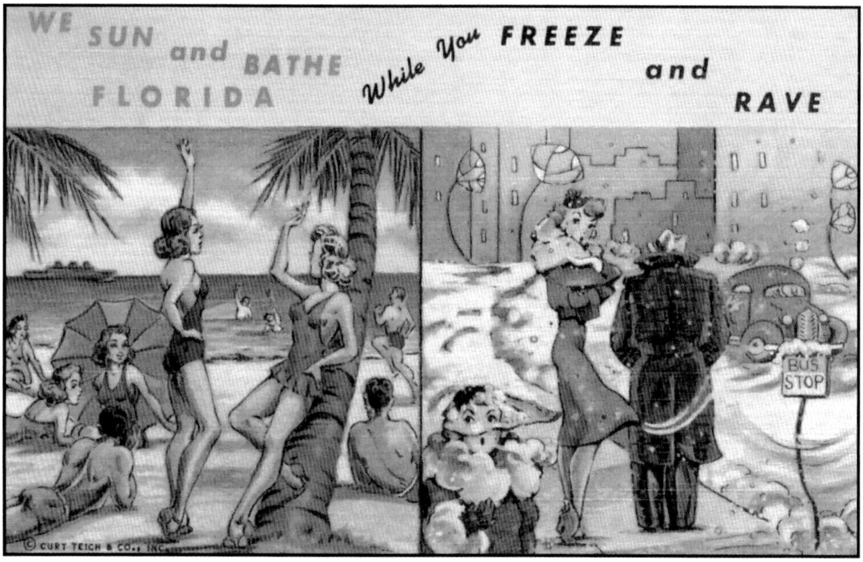

An illustrated postcard pokes fun at the unfortunate northerners who have to endure winter freezes.

Beginning in June 1934, St. Petersburg truly became the "Sunshine City" to weathermen and winter visitors. For the next eighteen months, the sun never failed to appear over the blessed city, saving Lew Brown of the *Independent* from giving away free newspapers and prompting yet another stroke of genius from Lodwick, the city publicity master.

He found it in the youthful faces of eight St. Petersburg toddlers.

"All Sunshine, No Clouds in their Young Lives," reported national newspapers, soaking up Lodwick's story of "Sunshine Babies." Cooing and smiling, one set of twin girls and six other tots' photos radiated above captions claiming, "All eight of them have been taught to walk and talk without a sunless day." For months, publications reprinted the article.

Lodwick needed the energetic editorials of St. Petersburg's "Sunshine Babies." His floating flop, the Goodyear blimp's arrival in St. Petersburg, spoiled an otherwise successful streak of selling St. Petersburg. The dirigible craze was comparable to the January 1914 inaugural flight across Tampa Bay, with Tony Jannus as the world's first commercial pilot—both had tremendous civic support, but the novelties soon wore out their welcome.

During the first ten months of 1935, St. Petersburg showed significant recovery as residential housing construction increased to match the throngs of new residents. In fact, reported the *Wall Street Journal* in December of that same year, "the strongest home-buying movement in the history of the resort is underway."

Play Ball!

Although lax in formal widespread advertising, St. Petersburg's chamber of commerce and its "army of specialists employed to exploit the sunshine" claimed over 150,000 guests for the 1934–35 tourist season. St. Petersburg's sunshine fever was nearly as contagious as the national pastime of baseball. And St. Petersburg had both.

Known locally as the "Ambassador of Baseball," Al Fielding Lang initiated the long tradition of spring training in the Sunshine City. Major-league ball clubs from the Phillies, Cardinals and Yankees practiced pitching and base stealing on the city's shores.

Al Lang came to St. Petersburg in 1910 for his health—his doctor told him he had six months to live. Perhaps he chose the city because he read Dr. W.C. Van Bibber's article in a medical journal that proclaimed the St. Petersburg

During a pause in spring training for the 1934 season, local fan Dick Mayes from nearby Brookesville is flanked at Waterfront Park by baseball greats Lou Gehrig (left) and Babe Ruth.

area the healthiest place in America. We don't really know, but in any event, it worked. Al lived another fifty years until he died of pneumonia at eighty-nine.

Lang, who was from Pennsylvania, attempted to get the Pittsburgh Pirates to train here in 1912 but was rebuffed by owner Barney Dreyfuss, who reportedly said, "You must think I am a damn fool to train in a whistle stop little one tank town."

Fearless of striking out, Al was successful in convincing manager Branch Rickey to bring the St. Louis Browns here in 1914 with an offer of free lodging and free rent. The first game against the Cubs, who traveled from Tampa by boat, was played in Coffee Pot Park. One hundred advertising signs lined the field, and over four thousand fans witnessed the beginning of spring training in St. Petersburg. Chicago won the game 3–2. Alas, after one year, the Browns departed, but that initial game marked the creation of Major League Baseball's first all-purpose training camp.

Undaunted, Lang persuaded the Philadelphia Phillies to train here in 1915, and they returned for three more years. It was during this time that Florida's Grapefruit League began ripening: Jacksonville was host to Connie Mack's Philadelphia Athletics, the Cubs were in Tampa, the St. Louis Cardinals trained in St. Augustine and the St. Louis Browns called St. Petersburg their springtime practice ground. This was a major coup. Al was named "Ambassador to Baseball" and elected mayor.

Stan "the man" Musial and Al Lang (right) entertain sports reporters by performing executive grounds keeper duties at Sunshine Park. The ball diamond would later be named in Lang's honor.

In 1922, the Boston Braves were lured to the city by the construction of Waterfront Field. The Braves stayed until 1937, when the St. Louis Cardinals came to town. Perhaps Lang's greatest triumph was convincing Colonel Jacob Ruppert, owner of the Yankees, to move here in 1924. This made St. Petersburg famous as the only city in America with two spring training teams. In addition, the area received extensive publicity from the New York media.

Throughout the years, there were many other triumphs for our "Ambassador to Baseball," who attended every World Series until 1957. Lang was truly the "Father of Spring Training."

"St. Petersburg thereafter was winter capital of baseball," local historian Walter Fuller noted, "and Florida stole the Spring baseball show from California, Texas and other western states."

Aside from baseball and green benches, Al Lang took the Bathing Beauties, an icon created from Florida boom-era ballyhoo, further than the likes of Miami's Carl Fisher or St. Petersburg's John Lodwick ever managed. The former Sunshine City mayor inadvertently helped take a somewhat seedy barelegged boardwalk contest to crowning heights.

Aware of St. Petersburg's success in promotions of parades and pageants and the efforts of local pageant guru Leonora Slaughter, civic boosters from New Jersey sought Lang's assistance. As her supervisor, Al Lang agreed to lend Leonora Slaughter for a few weeks to help revise a desperate Atlantic City spectacle. "Well, you ought to go up there and show them damn Yankees how to do a *real* job with a pageant," a grinning Lang advised Slaughter.

Well prepared by her heady days of working for the St. Petersburg Chamber of Commerce, Slaughter excelled in Atlantic City. On December 1, 1941, she accepted the position as executive director for the Miss America Pageant. She never lived in St. Petersburg again, making the Atlantic City assignment a lifelong pursuit and creating a modern-day dynasty known worldwide.

Al Lang earned rave reviews from the city and throngs of thankful benchwarmers. That praise was long lived. On February 8, 1960, the *Tampa Tribune* ran the obituary for "Mr. Baseball," noting that he "died here today just hours before the spring drills began in his hometown."

"It was in 1925," the *Tribune* reported, "that he scored his biggest success with the landing of the New York Yankees for his home town. The Yanks have trained here ever since.

"Lang persuaded the St. Louis Cardinals to train here in 1938, and one of his happiest years was in 1942 when the Yanks and the Cards played in the World Series."

The obituary concluded by pointing out that Lang also saw profit potential in other sports venues: "St. Petersburg, which still does not have a football stadium larger than its high school field, was urged by Lang in 1930 to follow the example of Miami which constructed the Orange Bowl. He predicted that Miami would receive at least $50,000 a year from the bowl."

As the 1930s were concluding, civic leaders pledged to open a new ball field in recognition of his achievements in advancing St. Petersburg. However, with a probable Second World War looming, the ballpark for Al Lang, as well as the boastings of John Lodwick, would have to wait.

As for the resort city of St. Petersburg, with the coming of the war, little would remain the same.

Chapter Three

WAR AND BEYOND

In the fall of 1939, spurred by Adolf Hitler's invasion of Poland, the Second World War began with Great Britain and France declaring war on Germany. Concentrated efforts at sea, including effective submarine campaigns against Britain-bound merchant ships, soon gave way to catastrophic waves of German offensives. Moving west and gaining Axis countries along his warpath, Hitler's retaliation for Germany losing the First World War demanded attention from the world at large.

Desperate for land and natural resources to continue military actions against China and certainly aware—if not in awe—of recent blitzkrieg campaigns in France, Belgium, Luxembourg and the Netherlands, Japanese officials signed the Tripartite Act with Germany and Italy in late 1940. Now able to occupy French Indochina and control trade to China, Japan could effectively construct military installations and wage war on the surrounding resource-rich regions and European colonial holdings in the Far East.

American requests for Japanese withdrawal were to no avail. Newly empowered minister of war General Hideki Tojo, unwilling to leave French Indochina, was past the point of negotiations. Consequently, Tojo set in action the plan of fleet commander in chief Admiral Isoroku Yamamoto for a "surprise offensive extending throughout the Pacific area."

Answering the Call

Meanwhile, in the United States, policy makers prepared for a likely entrance into the world war. By October 1940, President Franklin D. Roosevelt's signature on the Burke-Wadsworth Selective Training and Service Act—the first peacetime draft in U.S. history—made intervention all but imminent. Subjected to compulsory military service during the War Between the States and the First World War, American men heard the call to arms and again responded in impressive numbers.

Over the course of World War II, 10 million men nationwide between twenty and thirty-five years of age were drafted for military service; the majority were selected for the army. Impressive as that figure was, it dimmed in comparison to the additional 6 million men and women who volunteered for enlistment primarily into the navy, the marines, the coast guard and the army air corps.

Street corner recruiting centers like this U.S. Coast Guard station were a common prewar sight in downtown St. Petersburg.

In the Sunshine State, a quarter million of Florida's nearly two million residents responded to Roosevelt's rally. The St. Petersburg district enrolled nearly ten thousand local registrants in one day alone. Across Tampa Bay in Hillsborough County, over twenty thousand citizens would join the armed services. While military enlistments were on the rise in St. Petersburg, the chamber of commerce, citizens and civic leaders followed suit in preparing for the future.

By mid-July, chamber funds for tourist activities were estimated at over $100,000 for the upcoming 1941–42 season. City publicist John Lodwick continued peppering society papers with the local happenings "in the warmth of the subtropics, under blue skies, and in a setting of flowers in full bloom." Lodwick even predicted swelling tourist seasons in St. Petersburg nearing the half-million mark.

In addition to increasing their membership rolls with each wave of new residents, civic clubs and women's organizations prepared for "the duration" by expanding their activities. Thousands of other Bay Area residents—some determined, but most probably desperate—joined the migration north or flocked to the West, seeking their own "New Deal" in defense-related jobs. Understandably, many assumed and feared that there would be few war production caveats for industry-free St. Petersburg.

In 1942, federal and state government leaders and civic boosters in both northern and southern states put a unique spin on what the average patriotic citizen could do to aid the war effort. Northern residents not employed in critical war-related jobs were urged to rent out their homes to the men and women who were manufacturing bullets, bombs and boats. Some northern states went so far as to offer "bonus" gasoline ration coupons to those who were willing to pack up, drive south and agree to reside for the duration in the warmer, more fuel efficient Florida climate.

In special mail-away editions, both the *Times* and *Evening Independent* urged tourists to come to St. Petersburg as part of the war effort. The rationale was that for every family who left the northeastern states to spend the winter in Florida, there were hundreds of gallons of precious fuel oil that would become available for the nation's war machine. The publications argued that Florida's annual fuel oil usage averaged about 200 gallons per family while in the North, wintertime usage alone was nearly nine times greater at almost 1,800 gallons per family. To avoid potential criticism, the papers were savvy enough to also urge readers to share these special editions so paper could be conserved.

In September 1941, John Lodwick cut short his newspaper contact trip to northern cities to return home and issue a front-page warning to state and local government officials about gas rationing

REFUTE RUMORS MAIL IT AWAY EDITION

St. Petersburg Times

Refute Rumors MAIL IT AWAY EDITION

SECTION THREE — ST. PETERSBURG, FLORIDA, SUNDAY, NOVEMBER 1, 1942 — TWENTY-SEVEN

Don't Listen to the Rumorons

WE WANT MORE VISITORS

Sure Army's Here, But St. Petersburg Can House You, Too

Rooms Still Available For 60,000 Civilian Visitors

By Jack Thale

Listen, mister, who said St. Petersburg didn't have room for you and the Army, too?

Because he's a rumoron. He's as wrong as a sugar bowl in a restaurant.

THE FACTS

Sure the Army is here. You'll see them on the streets, in restaurants, at the movies—bronzed, clear-eyed soldiers from your home town and his. Men who know we've got a job to do and are doing their part. Men you'll be proud of.

Yes, they've taken over some of the hotels. Maybe 15 or 20.

But—and these are cold, hard facts taken from official records—that still leaves exactly 88 larger hotels of 20 or more rooms for you to pick from for accommodations for you and your family.

And then there are still that same for-rent houses, apartments, rooms, courts, cottage colonies and smaller "family" hotels that there have always been.

Yes, the Army is here, but we still want winter visitors and have accommodations for thousands. A city wide survey—and again these are cold, hard facts taken from responsible official sources—shows there are accommodations for an estimated 60,000 winter visitors here.

And, in spite of what you may have heard, the rents haven't gone sky high. They're still the same and they're going to stay at pre-war levels.

Because, in common with scores of other areas throughout the country, rent levels here have been "pegged" by the office of price administration. Even if they wanted to, landlords couldn't charge you any more than the rent they got for the same accommodations last March.

Everybody—especially the men who have been there—knows how war breeds rumors. In three minutes you can hear 30 tales, and probably 20 of them will be as imaginative as Gulliver's Travels.

THE FACTS

You may have heard we have a blackout every night and you have to feel your way through pitchblack streets or stay indoors.

Nothing to it. The street lights are still burning and you can window-shop your way past brightly-lighted showcases up and down the shopping district any night.

Maybe you've heard that huge areas of the city have been closed to civilians. *Sheer boloney. It is possible to go to any part of the city with no more restrictions than in normal times.*

Probably you've heard the beaches are closed to the public now, or that oil from sunken ships has made them unfit for use.

More boloney. The mile upon mile of beaches are still here, the sand is as white and warm and smooth as it ever was and you can sunbathe along any of them to your heart's content.

Maybe you've heard that our street cars and busses aren't running any more because we haven't the tools or materials to keep them up. Or that you can't ride on them because they're so crowded with soldiers.

That's more silly stuff. The city has even revised and added to the system to provide more efficient means of travel for the additional people who are using public transportation these days. And there's plenty of room for all.

Of course, there isn't space here to go into all the wild tales you may have heard about what happened to St. Petersburg when the Army moved in.

But these few examples and the true facts are typical—and there's probably no more truth in the other things you may have heard than there were in the rumors we've exploded here.

And, by the way, in case you're still skeptical about the hotel situation, here is a list of the hotels here having 20 or more rooms which have not been taken over by the government and are still available for civilian visitors:

Alden, Alida, Ames, Anchor Inn, Arcadale, Avalon.

Bainbridge, Ballard, Barker's Inn.

Bates, Belmont, Biltwell, Binnie, Boca Ciega Inn, Bon Harbor, Burlington, Butler Arms.

Cameo Court, Campbell Castle, Central, Chicago, Commodore, Cozy Inn, Crawford, Crescent, Cunningham.

Detroit, Earlene, Embassy, Essex House, Esther Bush, Fifth Avenue, Florida, Gilbert, Gordon, Gotham, Gregory, Harlan, Harden's.

Idlease.

Kranghurst.

Latonia, Lenox, Lucerne.

Macom, Manhattan, Marion-Franklin, Mercer, Merritt, Miller, Morrison.

Newman's, Oak Lodge, Owosso, Park House, Patton, Penn, Pennaflora, Pennaflora Rooms, Penn State, Plaza, Prince George.

[illegible], Rexmere, Richelieu, Ridgway House, Rockholm.

St. Charles, St. Petersburg, Seville, Shenandoah, [illegible].

South [illegible], Sunny Bay Manor, Sunset, Sunshine Inn, Suwannee.

Tides, West Coast Inn, White House Inn, Wilmer, Windsor, Wirick, Woodward.

A special mail-away edition of the *St. Petersburg Times* urged northerners in November 1943 to move to Florida for the duration of the war, emphasizing that the Sunshine City had plenty of accommodations for all.

The usually upbeat promoter spoke of gloom and doom, saying that because of gasoline embargos, potential visitors were fearful of being stranded on the highway if they attempted a motor trip to St. Petersburg.

"Florida stands to lose $10,000,000 in gasoline taxes this season and next year," Lodwick told the *Evening Independent*, "unless action is taken immediately to lift the curfew and embargo."

He warned that the loss of gas tax dollars would affect road building programs, public schools and, of course, tourism. Citing chamber of commerce statistics, he said between 72 and 75 percent of all tourists who visited St. Petersburg came by automobile, and the gasoline embargo would be disastrous.

"If Canada, at war, can relax its curfew [for American tourists,] I see no reason why the same cannot be done for our major industry, in time of peace," he argued with little success.

At the risk of sounding unpatriotic, Lodwick said the newspaper editors with whom he spoke did not believe that a claimed gas shortage was real.

"As soon as [energy secretary Harold] Ickes made public his ruling rationing gas, the Canadian government relaxed their curfew law for American tourists, Sundays included," Lodwick argued. "And they were frank in admitting the move was made for the sole purpose of stimulating tourist trade from the states."

Lodwick noted that summer travel to our northern neighbor was the "best since prohibition" and that the one saving grace for Florida might be the "soaring increase" that was taking place with railroad passenger service to the South.

"Americans wanting to travel this winter have all too few places to choose from, with the result being that St. Petersburg is once again in a position to enjoy a capacity season," the public relations pro claimed. "But there is heavy pressure work to be done immediately," he warned, "to protect state revenues from the sale of gas…and to assure motorists [that] plenty of fuel is available."

Boosters maintained in 1942 that even though the army had commandeered a huge number of St. Petersburg hotel rooms, nearly sixty thousand rooms were still available for tourists. The Lodwick-inspired concept was that despite hardships, Florida and particularly St. Petersburg was still a sunshine paradise.

That same year Vice-mayor Walfred Lindstrom, hotel association executive secretary Wilmer Sadler and civic booster William Kenmuir set out on a five-thousand-mile goodwill jaunt through Birmingham, Atlanta, Memphis,

New recruits stand at attention by their pup tents for a field inspection of their equipment in a beachside bivouac area near the St. Petersburg waterfront.

St. Louis, Indianapolis, Louisville, Fort Wayne, Chicago and Milwaukee to advertise the city's "available rooms" policy. The ambassador's message was simple and repeated almost as rapidly as a basic trainee's machine gun fire: "The Army is here, but we still have rooms for you!" They stressed that St. Petersburg had more than "100 hotels and 1,200 apartment houses available for tourists," not to mention the availability of cabins, campgrounds, cottages and private residences. They said St. Petersburg offered an ideal location for persons not directly involved in the war effort to make their homes, thus relieving conditions in already crowded defense areas. And they praised some northern states for promoting the "go to Florida" promotion; rationing boards in Connecticut, for example, were willing to increase gasoline allocations to many families who stated they would spend the entire winter in the Sunshine City.

William Kenmuir was one of the city's most sincere and energetic promoters. During his career, he made a total of twelve goodwill trips around the country. The former chamber of commerce president also excelled at organizing and staging much of the entertainment each winter season at Williams Park for both guests and residents.

Decked out in their white linen suits and Panama hat "uniforms," Vice-mayor Walfred Lindstrom (left) and civic booster William Kenmuir review a full-page *Evening Independent* ad promoting St. Petersburg.

Traveling by bus on this twelve-state jaunt, Kenmuir and his colleagues had a string of tickets nearly forty feet in length. The promoter's "uniform" was an unspoken homage to the eye-catching white suite and straw hat made famous by Frank Pulver and his flamboyant Purity League escapades.

Stack 'Em High, Sell 'Em Cheap

Ask any resident who lived in St. Petersburg prior to the Nixon administration about his or her favorite place to shop, and you will most likely be inundated with fond memories and grand tales of one place: Webb's City and its charismatic owner, James Earl "Doc" Webb.

With a growing bank account, Doc left Tennessee to become a managing partner in a friend's St. Petersburg drugstore in 1925. For the next year, the duo operated the Seaboard Drug Store (named for its proximity to the Seaboard rail line). Then came the bust of Florida's land boom.

Webb's partner, most likely nervous about the rapid decline in the economy, sold his portion of the store to Doc and headed back to the hills of Tennessee. Webb immediately began slashing prices to lure in cash-strapped customers. By 1932, Doc had incorporated the store as Webb's Cut Rate Drug Co. and topped $500,000 in sales. He topped the cool million mark four years later.

What began as a seventeen- by twenty-eight-foot storefront on the "wrong side of the tracks" in 1925 rapidly ballooned into a monolithic empire that took up nearly ten city blocks thanks to the vision of James Webb. "I don't give a damn about money; I want customers," he once declared in an interview. And did he ever get them—up to sixty thousand of them daily.

Always a fighter for the common man, Doc refused to raise prices and constantly ran advertisements announcing that he would undercut any competitor's price by 10 percent. It worked, sometimes too well. In fact,

Very much a serious businessman, James Webb was a hands-on entrepreneur involved in every aspect of his nationally known Webb's City. His motto was "stack 'em high and sell 'em cheap."

during a 1938 visit to the growing Webb's store, William Bristol of the Bristol-Myers Corp. became so enraged at Doc's low prices on its products that Doc found himself in court defending his rights to sell his goods at his own chosen price and not that of the manufacturer's suggested price. He won, although he would find himself in court many more times on similar supplier complaints.

Incorporated as Webb's City in 1946, Doc's empire flourished. As customers began requesting more items for purchase, Doc responded. Folks wanted gas and tires, so he opened a gas station next door. Folks wanted foodstuffs, so he opened a grocery store. Haircuts, sure, you can get one for fifty cents in the barbershop and get a free ice cream cone afterward. Doc sold it all. From carpet and cantaloupes to clothes and curtains, customers came in droves to visit dozens of different stores at Webb's City. And not just for the low prices. Always a salesman (and certainly a showman), Webb provided seemingly

The fun promotional side of Doc Webb found him riding elephants, posing with his always popular Poster Girls or hamming it up with his dog and a couple of clowns—anything to attract attention.

endless attractions. Mermaid shows, dancing chickens, bathing beauties and three-ringed circuses entertained weary mothers and restless children.

Gimmicks were Doc's forte. You never knew when a sale would happen or where. Want to save 20 percent on women's underwear? They're on sale at the cigar counter for the next five minutes. Once, he even sold one-dollar bills for ninety-five cents each. Anything to lure the customers in and to keep them shopping, which they did. Doc confidently proclaimed in a 1949 advertisement that "all roads lead to Webb's City."

The 1950s and 1960s were the golden decades for the "World's Most Unusual Drugstore." In 1970, Webb's City consisted of more than seventy individual stores in seven buildings with a total of three thousand parking spaces. Sensing a downturn in the economy and with the arrival of urban shopping malls, Webb sold his 56 percent share of the company to Texas interests in 1974. Perhaps the loss of its greatest promoter was too much for Webb's City, for it went into bankruptcy and closed a few years later, a sad day in St. Petersburg, for sure.

Prewar St. Petersburg was a charming southern city centered on the tourist trade. It was also a community still small enough to rent a two-bedroom apartment for only thirty-five dollars a month and to have residents like Rudolph LaVine and his wife stroll the hexagon-block sidewalks flanking downtown streets, treat themselves to a sidewalk vendor snack or just relax on the Sunshine City's famous green benches. "The outdoor watermelon stands were very popular," recalls Mrs. LaVine in a 1989 *Times* article. "On warm days we would ride to Central and Sixteenth [Streets] and get a quartered, ice-cold watermelon for 10 cents."

The celebrated green benches that graced the city's parks and sidewalks, however, had become noticeably vacant.

Following the Great Depression, pending war restrictions nearly delivered a knockout blow to the Sunshine City. War, continents away, threatened to destroy the very fabric of St. Petersburg's tourist-dependent economy. Like tourist-dependent Miami and Miami Beach, St. Petersburg was gearing up for the winter of 1941–42 tourist season when the news of Pearl Harbor made its way down the Florida shores. It was feared, for both destination cities, that inevitable war and governmental constraint would decimate the tourist dollars.

"There were very few tourists because of gas rationing," observed Mrs. LaVine, "and the military had priority on other means of transportation." Unknown to her and many others, this was only the beginning; a momentous change, more extensive and lasting, was on the horizon. Even with war imminent, John Lodwick remained confident that St. Petersburg could manage another successful season. It seemed little could dissuade him from selling the Sunshine City. Newspaper editors and columnist across America knew Lodwick's first love was St. Petersburg. Lauding his contributions locally, former mayor Al Lang went as far as stating, "No man ever did a greater work in publicizing the city."

Citizens respected Al Lang's judgment. After all, it was Lang's love of "America's favorite pastime" that brought baseball training to Florida. For decades to come, datelines of "Florida" and, more specifically, "St. Petersburg" appeared in sports pages nationwide. Both as mayor and a civic-minded citizen, Al Lang assisted in advancing St. Petersburg's image as a recreational paradise. It was through Lang that John Lodwick befriended Babe Ruth.

St. Petersburg loved the "Sultan of Swat." Stories abound of the Babe's kindness toward children and his love for all things excessive. Lodwick

Gas restrictions, war rationing and tight money cut dramatically into tourist revenues, and the city's green benches were obviously vacant.

scored even more points for the city when he staged a "surprise" birthday bash for Ruth.

On December 7, 1941, morning newspaper subscribers read John Lodwick's latest plug for his beloved city.

"What America needs this winter is an old-fashion nerve tonic," prescribed Lodwick, "and St. Petersburg has it." By midafternoon, however, as word of Pearl Harbor's bombing reached the States, vacationing in St. Petersburg (or anywhere for that matter) became a pill few could swallow.

The future seemed uncertain for many. For editors of the *St. Petersburg Times*, reflection on the past and future weighed heavily as 1942 rapidly approached. "The day has come," noted one such editorial, "when local business leaders, especially, are asking, 'Is this enough?' For many city officials and merchants, it was not. "They feel," continued the perspective, "that St. Petersburg is now large enough—thanks to the vision of the men who founded it—to be both a great resort center and to have industrial resources, as well."

Once again, the *St. Petersburg Times* championed for the city's survival through selling its resources.

Within six months of the attacks on Pearl Harbor, Midway, Guam and the Philippines, the clear skies and exotic terrain of Florida became military training grounds. By war's end, the government had laid over fifteen miles of highway, erected more than forty aviation bases and constructed the massive military installations and elaborate infrastructures required to house and support in excess of 1 million sailors, soldiers and airmen. From city-sized bases in Jacksonville to obscure bombing ranges in Sopchoppy, the Sunshine State housed over 170 military installations. Major defense contracts awarded to sparsely populated Florida came as a kick-start to a stalling statewide economy.

Through ample political persuasion by chamber and city leaders, aided by like-minded members of Congress and Florida's Hotel Commission, the city of St. Petersburg landed a coveted role in the war effort. With spacious skies, thirty-five miles of sandy beaches and mangrove-infused barrier islands, St. Petersburg was an ideal location for army air corp training and amphibious assault drills.

Coupled with plenty of vacant and nearly abandoned hotels, the city would practically hand over the keys and open its arms to the 100,000 plus servicemen. From hotel managers and local merchants to students and civic boosters, war efforts were widespread.

In Florida, and certainly St. Petersburg, public participation and civic volunteerism extended beyond housing and hospitals for military trainees.

As troops trained on the city's shores and barrier islands simulating the overseas battlefield, locals trained to assist in the fields at home. While plane spotting and bandage rolling were important to the nation's homefront war assistance, the nation's agriculture experts and farmers feared for future crops.

Women at War

During the summer of 1942, panic set in when farmers began taking into account the absence of nearly six million agriculture workers. Rich in citrus, cotton, tobacco, sugarcane, phosphate, turpentine and cattle ranching, Florida's rural economy depended heavily on external labor. Farmers across the nation found themselves in a crisis and in need of immediate attention. With an estimated shortage of ten thousand agriculture workers, Florida fields were no different. Chambers of commerce and civic clubs formed organizations like the Crop Corps and the Women's Land Army to seek out willing hands. Most of those available to work were women.

By September 1942, *Independent Woman* had published Elizabeth Spense's article "War Time Harvest" to remind us that "America's 1942 Food-For-Freedom campaign would be incomplete without special mention of the gallant service of women, a service which may well be the decisive factor in America's food production campaign." Other women in the Tampa Bay area filled war-vacated positions such as bus and streetcar operators, auto mechanics and bank tellers. Many of these women not only worked in war jobs at Tampa shipyards as welders and riveters but also managed families and households and volunteered to do more for the cause. Not since World War II has any event produced so many opportunities for so many women.

Whether women volunteered due to the same patriotism and propaganda that made Joan of Arc and her famous muscle-flexing sister Rosie find war jobs or because of finances, companionship and pride in learning new skills is unclear. On the St. Petersburg homefront, however, volunteering empowered countless women with an invigorated sense of independence, identity and individuality. In short, notes historian Gary Mormino, "World War II served as a great watershed for American women."

An intense nationwide campaign to "sell the war" created "supercharged atmospheres of patriotism and sacrifice" that relied heavily on civic support and local volunteerism, says Mormino. Public policy and propaganda

If it hadn't been for the WASPs—the civilian Women Airforce Service Pilots—many newly built bombers would have been delayed in getting from the factory to military bases and into battle. Carrying their parachutes (left to right), Frances Green, Margaret Kirchner, Ann Waldner and Blanche Osborn leave their B-17 after ferry training at an army air force base in Ohio.

efforts were instrumental in defining the "new woman's role." Empowered by current circumstances, women were no longer "the helpless victims as portrayed in the photography of the progressive era."

Modest groups of well-to-do women, who often made assisting others a career, were the primary volunteers and social organizers prior to the turn of the twentieth century. It was not until much later that a different kind of volunteer work evolved. Associations began making use of thousands of working and middle-class women on a part-time basis in activities such as PTA committees, Boy and Girl Scouts, community improvement organizations and fundraising. In addition to these social and civic committees, women were asked to gather resources to meet immediate military needs through conserving sugar, coffee, shoes, rubber and fuel, among other things. It was the rationing of food, however, that affected the stomachs of every citizen.

Propaganda and publicity campaigns not only targeted women for gardening and food preservation but also urged every man, woman and child to push, pull or drag salvageable materials to donation points. Urgent and consistent reinforcement of daily salvage habits suggested that every bottle, bone and scrap of aluminum or tin would win the war.

Articles of clothing that could be mended, patched or stitched into something else not only provided consumer savings but also freed the manufacturing industry to produce those goods for the war effort.

St. Petersburg women were also active in service recreation clubs, such as the Bomb-a-Dears. Patriotic young women of St. Petersburg entertained, danced with and provided companionship for local soldiers—of course, not until after "furnishing references acceptable to the Defense Mothers as to their moral characters," according to Mrs. Stuart Warren in a January 1, 1943 *Times* article.

Not all promotions and publicity, however, pushed for bond drives, recycling and citizen support. Playing off the prevalent rationing theme, St. Petersburg's chamber members suggested a trip to St. Petersburg to "Get your Sunshine Quota." "Now, as ever before, it is important for all Americans to keep health and energy in high gear," the chamber declared.

In fact, other advertisements asserted, "St. Petersburg is America's Sunshine base for freedom" and "Get your Vitamin 'V' for Victory at Sunny St. Petersburg." Although the government had taken over all but one of the Sunshine City's major hotels, the Suwannee, there were plenty of available accommodations, assured city boosters.

"If you are not in war work, save fuel, protect your health and live in the sunshine," said chamber of commerce ads. Moreover, the solicitations stated, there is "No Rationing of Sunshine and Hospitality."

Writing as the "voice of the traveler" for the *New York Times* and the *Chicago Daily Tribune*, John Lodwick dismissed rationing's impact on tourism, noting that St. Petersburg's efforts to ensure an active resort atmosphere contributed to the "national morale so essential to the successful prosecution of the war."

Death of a Salesman

On October 16, 1942, as the death toll overseas continued rising, the city of St. Petersburg lost one of its own. Slumping forward in his seat aboard a city streetcar, John Harris Lodwick, director of city publicity, died suddenly from an apparent heart attack. Local radio station WTSP issued two morning bulletins informing the city that "the man who had organized and headed St. Petersburg's municipal publicity department for more than two decades, had succumbed."

His widow, Margaret, and former mayor Frank Pulver read the tribute plaque to John Lodwick dedicated in 1951 to honor America's first municipal publicity director. *Courtesy of the* Tampa Bay Times.

Lodwick's death at fifty-two years of age came as a shock to citizens and civic leaders alike. By one o'clock that afternoon, mourning the loss of "the pioneer booster," chamber of commerce doors closed for the day.

Survived by wife Margaret Guinter Lodwick, his mother and nine siblings—all from Ohio as well—John Lodwick was laid to rest a few days later. At the overflowing Rhodes Chapel in St. Petersburg, friends and former associates gathered to pay respect to the "man who had spread the fame of the city far and wide."

Speaking at his funeral, Wyman Willingham, president of the chamber of commerce, commended Lodwick's contributions. "Records reveal that the per capita cost of advertising and publicity in bringing winter visitors here is the lowest on record," noted Willingham. "This is a tribute to the genius of Lodwick in his ability to obtain much valuable publicity throughout the country at practically no cost." Other tributes to Lodwick portrayed him in a fitting manner.

City manager Glenn V. Leland had this to say of St. Petersburg's first publicity director:

> *He gave his full time to his work and was instrumental in publicizing the city to the extent that it has become known as one of the nation's leading resort centers. The length of his service in this capacity gained him a host of friends among northern newspapermen and accounted for hundreds of columns of city publicity which otherwise would have been impossible to obtain…a service that only a few men could have duplicated.*

St. Petersburg had lost a founding father that fall, yet it managed to proceed forward with its goal of selling itself. By the following summer, the city advertising committee brought to the table an aggressive campaign to bring additional winter residents and new industries. With a proposed $50,000 budget, $15,000 more than the previous season, boosters aimed to promote the city in more than thirty-five leading newspapers, magazines and trade publications. The detailed plan sought a circulation figure well over eleven million. Stating that there were more than seven million American citizens over the age of sixty-five, suggestions were made "that these people can do the country a service by coming to St. Petersburg this winter, conserving their own health, saving fuel, and making more room in northern defense areas for essential war workers."

Local advertising agents listed three classes of tourists sought for vacationing in St. Petersburg. The first were the elderly or those unfit for the military or war production work at home, followed by those in ill health requiring the sunny and therapeutic climes of the Sunshine City. Lastly, families of soldiers and children "who need a warm climate during the winter months" would be targeted. But boosting St. Petersburg's annual winter tourist figures was not all that the chamber of commerce had in mind.

In late June 1943, chamber governors announced plans to advertise St. Petersburg during the annual Lions International Convention in Cleveland, Ohio. Members also requested a tally of available rooms and hotels for let in preparation for their next drive to encourage war workers and servicemen to call St. Petersburg home. By September, revised figures estimated 50 million persons through nearly sixty newspapers and magazines would read of the upcoming fall advertising campaign.

The Cunard cruise line office in Chicago frequently looked more like the northern Sunshine City promotion headquarters, thanks to attractive storefront displays.

The chamber's new "Come See St. Petersburg this Season, If You Can" campaign curtailed the use of color ads for fear of promoting travel for luxury, which the government highly discouraged. Even the word "winter visitors" replaced "tourists" for the duration. Calculating that the prewar tourist seasons had been bringing nearly a quarter million visitors, each spending around $200, boosters estimated a $50 million benefit to the city: "Figuring the value of the tourist trade as $50,000,000 during a season, the $50,000 spent for advertising represents a cost of only one-tenth of 1 per cent of the results." This was a figure even John Lodwick, the king of free publicity, would have appreciated.

Pictures Through a Wire?

Typhoon damage in Okinawa and a bear hunt in Cadillac, Michigan, were two of the front-page stories in the Monday, October 11, 1948 edition of the *St. Petersburg Times*, an issue that would have had the late John Lodwick celebrating and planning his next picture promotion of the city he loved. The *Times* had just joined the Associated Press wire photo network, which enabled it to send and receive photos literally worldwide in a matter of hours rather than days or weeks by conventional mail.

To today's social media generation, the wire photo technology seems more primitive than a horse and buggy. But for the first time ever, "the latest news" was at the corner newsstand or on your front porch. Sports fans could see pictures of yesterday's big play instead of just reading a play-by-play description. One can only imagine what would have been going through Lodwick's mind had he been among the readers viewing the AP wire photos of the fifth game of the '48 World Series between the Boston Braves and Cleveland Indians. The action shots were the first three images to be received by the *Times.* Oh, the promotion possibilities!

Calling it "the super miracle of 1946," the *Miami Daily News* led all Florida newspapers in adopting the wire photo technology and was closely followed by publications in Jacksonville, Tampa, Orlando and, finally, St. Petersburg.

As explained to *Times* readers, it took about eight minutes to scan a photograph for transmission, which could then be sent to any or all of the wire photo network subscribers, anywhere in the world. On the receiving end, it took about the same length of time to produce line-by-line an image suitable for printing.

In 1907, the *Scientific American* had published on its cover the first photograph ever successfully transmitted over a telegraph line. But nearly two decades would pass before the technology was refined and put into daily use, radically changing newspaper publishing.

The Associated Press started its wire photo service in January 1935, sending photos to thirty-nine newspapers in twenty-five cities. It revolutionized how news and human-interest pictures could be distributed. Writer and meteorologist Mark Monmonier, in his book *Air Apparent*, says newspapers subscribing to the AP service had the added benefit of receiving two daily weather maps, one for morning publication and a second updated version for afternoon dailies. Forecasting became more timely and accurate and a commodity that many newspapers regularly promoted to their readers.

Through his city public relations occupation and his own John Lodwick News Service, the tireless promoter introduced users of the Polk City directory to the beauties of St. Petersburg.

By the mid-1950s, more than five hundred publications subscribed to either the AP or United Press International services, and wild theories about using satellites for worldwide communication were rapidly evolving. And the St. Petersburg stories—complete with bathing beauties—could now easily and quickly reach travel magazines and newspapers in virtually any country.

Prior to the AP and UPI achieving international status in the wire service industry, smaller co-op news services filled the demands of editors as best they could.

Creating the John Lodwick News Service, an enterprise apparently run in addition to his city and chamber duties, may have caused a rift with some of the St. Petersburg Chamber of Commerce leadership, but Lodwick was certainly ahead of his peers in the public relations industry doing it the old-fashioned way; he worked for it. His news service even managed to place an enticing cheesecake photo in the respected R.L. Polk City Directory.

The *Times* Wide-World Pictures Syndicate in 1927 had more than one hundred St. Petersburg scenes on file—hand delivered by Lodwick on one of his many goodwill trips—ready at a moment's notice for their syndicated distribution. On one of several promotional trips north, Lodwick met with sports and features editors to discuss exactly the kind of material they were interested in publishing. Lodwick went so far as to arrange for office space in St. Petersburg for *New York Telegram* sports editor Joe Williams during the Yankees spring training season. At the same time, Lodwick and the H.J. Conover Features syndicate made final arrangements for coverage of the Lipton Cup sailing races to be staged in St. Petersburg.

The tireless PR man always received a warm welcome in particular from cities and towns scattered across Michigan. Favorite hangouts of the rich and beautiful people included fashionable Benton Harbor, Traverse City and a shuffleboard-crazy following from the village of Petoskey on the shores of Lake Michigan. Lodwick promised most editors "exclusives," which he made good on because, in reality, no one in Trenton, New Jersey, wanted to read about Mr. and Mrs. Smith from Detroit enjoying their sunshine state vacation. But readers of the *Detroit Herald* wanted exactly that kind of homespun news, and Trenton got stories about its locals too.

Despite an economic downturn, St. Petersburg tourism in 1936 broke all previous records registering fifty thousand signed-in guests at the chamber of commerce. Newspaper stories published the names of most of the four hundred plus who registered in just one day, with visitors from New York leading the count. Guests from Pennsylvania, Indiana and Ohio were among the next top finishers in that order for the day. It was clear that the marketing blitz aimed at these states was paying off and news services were aiding in that effort.

With these new official registrations in hand, John Lodwick and his assistant, Pressley Phillips, had plenty of publicity ammunition for a growing list of hometown newspapers: a posed photo of Mr. and Mrs. Harry B. Shields of Terra Haute enjoying a "balmy sun filled day on the beach in St. Petersburg" was mailed to Indiana two days after the Shieldses signed in at the chamber welcoming center. That particular week, the Shieldses were joined by tourists from twenty-five other states, the District of Columbia and Canada.

Pressley Phillips, fittingly nicknamed "Press," succeeded the affable Lodwick upon his death in 1942 and continued for the next nineteen years to exercise some of the Lodwick techniques that drew so much attention to the Pinellas Peninsula. He benefitted considerably from the close working relationship he had with a cadre of creative photographers such as Bob Preston, Carlton Gould and Jack Swenningsen and, of course, the new photo wire service technology.

Like Lodwick, Jack Swenningsen was a master of stage work. "My station wagon had any prop imaginable. Red towels, beach balls, wax fruit, bikinis, shorts, paper flowers, rods, reels, you name it." While Gould was capturing the city's beautiful people and pageantries, "I was known for set-up photography," Jack recalled with pride some sixty years later.

After more than sixty years of photography, Jack Swenningsen is now a convert to digital technology, but he fondly recalls the bulky Speed Graphic camera days that gave the shooter only one sheet of four- by five-inch film at a time and just one chance to "get the shot." *Photo by Scott Keeler; courtesy of the* Tampa Bay Times.

Like so many before him, Swenningsen came to Florida to escape the blistering winds of the north. "After the war, I returned to New York for two years. In 1948, I had a wife and two kids…we were all suffering, so I said, 'Florida, here we come.'" And he never regretted it.

To set up a calendar shot like this required fish, and Jack bought his "catch" from a local market, which knew him as "the crazy camera guy that wants the heads left on." *Photo courtesy Jack Swenningsen.*

"I was in utopia, and it was a lot different than Brooklyn. Two days later, I had a job with Florida Speaks. I told them I was the 'Picture Man' and was hired on the spot," Swenningsen said. He soon connected with Carlton Gould and Pressley Philips, who ran the publicity department for the chamber. "We sold pictures by the droves, and in those days, they were paying $1.10 per 8 x 10." Not bad money for a photographer in those days, he boasted.

"Gould did primarily cheesecake shots and was connected with the city's Charm School. We'd call them up and ask them to send us some girls and their boyfriends." To Jack, the subject may have not been as important as the set-up and the selling of St. Petersburg as a year-round Sunshine City.

"I wasn't satisfied with the 'ordinary' shot. I would plan it to the 'T' and capture with one great shot." He shot hundreds, if not thousands, of photos for local attractions, motels, hotels and merchants throughout the state. At ninety-seven, Jack noted much had changed thanks to digital photography.

These days, anyone with a digital camera can take dozens upon dozens of shots and will most likely capture one worth publishing, but not ole Jack.

"We sold pictures by the droves," said Jack, noting that on occasion, his daughter served as an attractive model, with a leg up on the competition. *Photo courtesy Jack Swenningsen.*

"They called me 'One Shot Swenningwhistle'…If I couldn't do it in one shot…maybe two… then no one could."

Not only was he saving film, he was saving his clients' money. Hoteliers loved when he would use multiple images on a single postcard, thus reducing production and advertising costs. Many of these postcards pictured the

During a relaxed conversation on his front porch, the ninety-seven-year-old photographer reminisced about this classic Mr. Sun "set-up" photo depicting almost every recreational activity available in St. Petersburg. "See those water skiers and that sailboat?" he proudly asked. "That didn't just happen; they were hired, too. I had to shoot when they were exactly in the right place." *Photo courtesy Jack Swenningsen.*

obligatory pretty gal, stretches of white sandy beaches and, of course, the larger than life Mr. Sun.

A great prop that said it all, Mr. Sun was the brainchild of Griffin Advertising, and Jack took it to a new level. Using marine-grade plywood, Jack took the smiling, comical Mr. Sun from a simple drawing to a six-foot-diameter advertisement.

Painted in enamel and so large it had to be strapped to the top of his station wagon, Jack rarely missed a chance to place it in the shot. Lodwick would have been proud and perhaps a bit envious of this technique. For Jack, he was just sharing his love of photography, St. Petersburg and a great set-up. "Boy, I wonder what happened to that old sign."

Reel Promotion and Readjustment

Aside from the city's quest for additional visitors and residents through printed publications, local Rotary members introduced a new medium of advertising. The dawn of promotional films had arrived. Using "technicolor" film, city boosters traveled to Indiana, where the motion picture was widely shown before Valparaiso Rotary members. So captivating was the film, audience members "could almost conjure in their minds" the wide, white sandy beaches and images of friends resting on the city's green benches. Scores of films, many produced for the city by Skylark Productions, featured the likes of Ma and Pa Sawyer, from any town USA, living life to the fullest in the Sunshine City.

Sunshine played the title role in many of these pseudo-documentaries with announcer Burrell Smith "inviting *you* to come along as we go once more in search of that which is interesting and exciting."

Back in the day when TV stations started their broadcast days at noon or even later in the afternoon and signed off before midnight, a St. Petersburg native son was working his way to becoming one of the pioneers in the exciting new industry. Burrell Smith graduated from St. Petersburg High School in 1935, attended St. Petersburg Junior College and later studied at Columbia University in New York City. As soon as he saw his first television broadcast, he knew he wanted to be a filmmaker.

Becoming a jack-of-all-trades in this brand-new field called broadcasting, he was instrumental in making St. Petersburg one of the first cities in the nation to advertise on both the small and big screen via short ten- to fifteen-minute matinee feature films. Smith formed Major Films, Inc., and became proficient at scriptwriting, narration and directing for promotional and educational films. His folksy story-telling approach was well accepted by station managers hungry for new and entertaining material to broadcast.

Like John Lodwick before him, Smith went to the chamber of commerce leaders and "sold" them on the idea of underwriting a series of promotional films about the Sunshine City. He convinced chamber promotional manager Joe Frohock in 1950 to push through a budget for a film program. In many cases, his film shorts were used by chamber officials in their presentations to travel societies, business groups and other civic gatherings, adding a new touch of excitement to the old tried and true—and often boring—slide shows.

Ruth Leatherman, a longtime chamber secretary, said she was particularly fond of Smith's series of special films under the title of *Home in the Sun*, featuring local beaches, the Festival of States celebration, Major League Baseball spring training and tours of city parks. It was also claimed that Smith was the first to bring film coverage of local Greyhound dog racing to the big screen, turning a young canine named Denied into a four-legged star, seen by thousands of moviegoers across the Midwest.

After the city-owned television station WSUN went on the air in 1953, many of Smith's films became standard programming material, according to Dayton Saltsman, one of the first announcers to work at the station. The St. Petersburg chamber negotiated a deal with the Florida Development Commission to make copies of the Smith films available for distribution to TV stations on a national request basis. As a result, millions got to visit the Sunshine City while sitting on the couch in their own living rooms.

Among his last films, and the one Burrell Smith considered his best, was a fifteen-minute featurette entitled *Sunny Skyway*, which took viewers back in history to the first Spanish visitors and through history up to the completion of the original Sunshine Skyway Bridge in 1954.

In a review of nearly two dozen such films, the word "sun" or "sunshine" appeared in almost every title. From *Fun in the Sun* and *Liquid Sunshine* to *Sunny Days* and *Life Under the Sun*, the films portrayed St. Petersburg's attractions and accommodations as the ideal winter playground. Had John Lodwick been around for the introduction of these films at lodges and Rotary Clubs countrywide, he might have very well embraced the medium, discarding his pen and paper for reels of celluloid film.

Lodwick also missed seeing the seeds of his labors come into fruition following the events of late 1945.

The war's end was welcome news for all.

Miriam Mullins, a cadet nurse at nearby Mound Park (now Bayfront Medical Center), was training to aid the war effort. While studying in her room on that memorable day in August, Miriam heard the excited clamor of students and bolted for the door.

She and her roommate were among the first to reach First Avenue South and Fifth Street, where, outside the *St. Petersburg Times* building, they received one the of first newspapers "proclaiming the wonderful news." It was then that Miriam realized "the war had finally come to an end."

After allied forces secured victory in Europe and the Pacific and the confetti covering the streets of St. Petersburg was gone, the peninsula's mighty military complex all but vanished. St. Petersburg, with an impressive substructure and a booming citizenship, was reborn. As of 1940, Florida was the least populated southern state and ranked only twenty-seventh nationally. Eventually, the World War II occupation of Florida came to include the hundreds of thousands wives, girlfriends and children who trailed servicemen.

The Sunshine State had created enough fond memories for families, veterans and retirees to prompt a return en masse, prepping Florida for a twenty-first-century showdown with New York for a third-place population ranking. By 1950, the massive numbers that settled in St. Petersburg would double its sixty thousand prewar population census.

In addition to a hero's welcome, returning GIs received government gratitude in a modified version of the New Deal. Aside from disability and educational assistance, the Servicemen's Readjustment Act of 1944 included home loan guarantees, unemployment aide and, more significantly, job preference in the civil service sector with the right to reclaim prewar jobs.

Massive war production efforts throughout Florida left miles of improved public roads and extended highways, to which soaring numbers of Americans and their automobiles readily flocked. With new pavement under their tires and paid vacation time in their pockets, visitors descended on Florida in record numbers. For millions of retirees and returning GIs, newly enacted legislation offered a new life—and why not start it in sunny Florida, thought many. The tourism machine geared up for a heady run. At the same time citizens' and tourists' income levels rose, so did transportation methods.

The age of the commercial airline industry, while not necessarily new to Florida, was an added amenity for the tourist trade. The accessibility and great speeds possible with air travel allowed for less time on the journey and more time spent at the destination, wherever it may be. Florida propelled to the top of destination choices.

By war's end, as registration rates at the chamber of commerce soared, St. Petersburg held honor to such a coveted standing. City boosters, citing American Automobile Association assertions that "more of its members traveled in and out of St. Petersburg than any other Florida city," claimed the "State Tourist Crown." John Lodwick would have been pleased.

St. Petersburg's population figures had also increased dramatically by 1945. Following the war's end, more than eighty-five thousand people claimed the city as their permanent residence. Well over seven thousand of them, along with dignitaries far and wide, turned out to honor Al Lang the following spring. With the armistice signed, Al Lang had finally received his greatest honor. The dedication of "Albert F. Lang Field" that spring was yet another indication the city was ready for continued growth as a resort city of pleasure.

A Charming Opportunity

The war in Europe and the Pacific was finally over. Soldiers and sailors no longer trained on Tampa Bay shores or Gulf of Mexico beaches, and St.

Another creative two-for-the-price-of-one promotional photo seen by millions of magazine readers. Pressley Phillips coaches Charm School students on proper posture while balancing—what else?—Florida grapefruit, of course.

Peterburg's hotels were once again tourist accommodations instead of GI barracks and classrooms.

But on the last weekend in November 1947, had you been on a morning stroll past Al Lang baseball stadium or along Jaycee Beach, you would have witnessed a company of women doing basic training calisthenics. True, the uniforms were one- or two-piece bathing suits, and there were no guns or khaki uniforms in sight. But there was a great deal of shooting—with cameras, that is. These were the women of the St. Petersburg Charm School, class of '48, working on their fitness and their photogenic appeal.

A small handful of righteous residents complained that the beauty and poise training was risqué. One letter-to-the-editor writer alleged it was just "a dirty old man scheme" cooked up by photographers Carlton Gould,

Pressley Phillips and their camera club buddies to look at pretty women. In reality, the innovative Charm School, sponsored and operated by the city, was a valuable education resource for young women, as well as a very shrewd marketing strategy. The ten-week school garnered international attention from Canada to Australia and all points in between as yet another "first" for a municipally owned and operated enterprise.

Initially offered to young women ages sixteen to twenty-one, the first class drew more than four hundred young ladies intent on "properly improving themselves." Free classes were conducted on proper hair care, poise, make-up, posture and diet. The school offered four Saturday afternoon classes at Al Lang field and three midweek sessions at the YMCA under the direction of professional ballet artist Kathleen Galvin. Gould taught classes on proper techniques of posing before the camera and that same year produced the Miss St. Petersburg Beauty Pageant, which featured one hundred Charm School graduates. After two successful seasons, Press Phillips told the city's women's club that the Charm School publicity played a huge role in "selling St. Petersburg as a good place to live, own a home and rear a family."

At the time, *Collier's Magazine* was among the top glossy publications in the country. When the St. Petersburg Charm School was featured as the magazine's cover story, circulation exceeded 2 million readers. Paramount, MovieTone and Fox all produced feature films about the Charm School that were shown in theaters nationwide for several years in the early 1950s. Reporter George Bartlett claimed that in 1953 alone more than eight thousand "student body" photographs appearing in 1,200 daily newspapers, 1,000 weekly newspapers and 60 magazines were viewed by an estimated 40 million readers from Maine to California. And all of this was free advertising for the city of sunshine.

The Peachcake Lensman

Carlton Goodwin Gould Jr. called himself a "society photographer," but for a handful of years following World War II, most everyone called him the St. Petersburg camera guy; and in later years, they simply called him "Pops." From 1946 to 1949, Gould worked under the direction of Pressley C. Phillips, the city's publicity department director. In that capacity, Carlton captured images that clearly proclaimed, "St. Petersburg, sunshine and beauty." His photographs of both local and visiting fishermen hauling in the big ones were featured in newspaper sports sections across America. Weekly mailings of beauty queen shots and pristine beaches filled with frolicking bathing beauties made features editors happy for yet another day.

Gould's professional snapshots of family picnics, sailing and sunsets inspired thousands of readers to come to St. Petersburg to become temporary sun worshipers. His pictures of the gaily decorated cars and floats in the annual Festival of States parade went to literally every state or commonwealth in the nation. That festival replaced the annual George Washington birthday celebration and had been eagerly promoted by John Lodwick; it was subliminal propaganda at its finest. A float representing Michigan or Pennsylvania told snowbirds from those states not only that they were they welcome in St. Petersburg but also that they were special. At peak times, there were as many as two dozen active state societies, organized by and for visiting tourists. The chamber guest registration center urged folks to become active in these clubs as a way of making St. Petersburg feel even more "like their home away from home."

Gould and his wife, a high school French teacher, lived on Thirtieth Street South during the ideal Florida winter months but would retreat to the cooler climes of Portsmouth, New Hampshire, when summer humidity hit the Pinellas Peninsula. There, Gould still viewed the world through a camera lens and took pictures of the social elite at the luxury Wentworth-by-the-Sea Hotel. He captured images of celebrities such as Annie Oakley and Gloria Swanson at the historic and very exclusive resort. New England historian J. Dennis Robinson notes that nearly ninety of Carlton Gould's photographs, including those of a visiting Richard Nixon in 1963, are part of the large Smith Collection at the Portsmouth Athenaeum, a well-known repository of New Hampshire history.

To keep a ready supply of beautiful young women eager to be photographed, Gould helped organize the St. Petersburg Camera Club. Shutterbug enthusiasts—mostly male—held various classes, exhibits and competitions, among them a beauty contest for young women ages sixteen to twenty-two seeking the coveted title of Queen of Hearts. The honor was fittingly bestowed at Sunken Gardens on Valentine's Day 1949.

Just before Christmas 1950, with thermometers reading in the low teens, the *New York Times* travel section featured not one, not two, but three articles all supplied by the untiring St. Petersburg publicity department. A lengthy article about Florida's west coast and St. Petersburg was accented by a Gould photo of seagulls and pelicans hovering around Recreation Pier. Meanwhile, the *New York Journal-American* published a full-page photo and story about

The Peachcake Lensman (aka Carlton Gould) stands at his tripod ready to capture another cheesecake pose as other Charm School grads wait their turns in front of the lens.

Sally Robinson, a graduate of the city-owned Charm School that Gould helped organize and operate. The enthusiastic *Journal* reporter also gave Gould credit as having designed the bathing suit worn by the picturesque beauty, a questionable claim at best. Nevertheless, the newspaper ran his photo next to a typical northern snow scene, with the caption, "Some like it hot…some like it cold."

In May 1947, Gould and Dick Venning organized the Tarpon Ball at the Coliseum, featuring 125 Charm School grads. The event included the crowning of Miss St. Petersburg, qualifying her for the Miss Florida Beauty Pageant competition. Even though the contest was intended to showcase beautiful eighteen- to twenty-eight-year-old women who lived in St. Petersburg, the still-to-come 1970s baby boomer concept of "everybody gets a participation trophy" had already taken hold. The contest was intended to judge a young woman's poise, personality, intelligence, charm and beauty. Entrants were expected to have talent, "Such as singing, dancing or dramatic ability." However, the rules were broadened to include the rest

Following publication in countless newspapers, dozens of Piper Cub aircraft owners across the country contacted the chamber of commerce to request a copy of this classic Gould pin-up photo of Ann Rutherford, Miss Aviation 1947.

of 'em, Organizers announced that "girls unable to qualify for the Miss St. Petersburg contest may enter the pageant and be featured in a variety of stunts, drills and special acts."

As glamorous as all of this may sound, there was a twist to how Carlton Gould viewed his own success. In 1956, he earned the publishing credit of which he was most proud. Here was a guy that had probably photographed more than three thousand beautiful Sunshine City girls in all sorts of settings—some logical like playing in the surf, others a little far-fetched with a swimsuit-clad beauty demonstrating a kitchen table and set of chairs. But the photo honor that "Pops" Gould had earned wasn't for cheesecake shots at all; he was selected to have one of his photographs published as a full-page spread in the popular *U.S. Camera Annual*. The award-winning shot was a pelican. Later that same year, *U.S. Camera* magazine published a flattering three-page article about Gould, calling him "the Peachcake Lensman" and praising him for his uncanny ability to favorably present the Sunshine City to the rest of the world.

Bridge Building

When the Bee Line Ferry started operations, St. Petersburg was home to fewer than forty thousand residents. Hand-laid bricks lined the streets, tent cities spotted the city and crewman Early J. McMullen shuttled tourists and travelers across Tampa Bay. In 1934, Early J. McMullen Jr. joined his father's crew. After several years of performing yeoman's duty, Early Jr. followed his father's example and obtained a captain's license. But the arrival of World War II temporarily split the father-and-son team. Since the U.S. Army Air Corps controlled the ferries during the war, the elder McMullen assisted his country by transporting locals and soldiers from Tampa to MacDill Army Air Field.

In 1947, voters approved a $15 million construction bond issue that mandated that all monies repaid come from tolls collected, not from taxes raised.

By 1950, the city hosted a blowout event that Fourth of July revealing the new name for the Sunshine Skyway Bridge. The daylong patriotic celebration was highlighted by the opening of construction bids

The massive bridge was designed to "withstand hurricanes of all known intensities." Towering nearly fifteen stories above the bay, the elevated structure provided a 750-foot-wide passage for ships crossing Tampa Bay, thus eliminating the need for a drawbridge.

On Labor Day 1954, Governor Charley Johns officially opened the bridge to thousands of waiting automobiles and their excited passengers. By midnight, fifteen thousand autos had spanned the waters. What once took over an hour was now a short ten-minute drive.

Wartime Dream Boat Draws Attention

Older readers may recognize the name Rube Goldberg as the Pulitzer Prize–winning cartoonist famous for illustrations of how to accomplish simple tasks in an extremely complicated way. For example in one invention, a turtle bumps into a bowling ball causing it to roll over a lever that strikes a match that lights a candle that burns a string tied to a mannequin's arm that swivels upward and turns on a light switch. Goldberg ultimately enjoyed a sixty-year career as the wacky inventor of complex silly machines that did it the hard way.

On staff at the *St. Petersburg Times* in the 1950s was another man named Rube—Rube Allyn, who did equally wacky things in order to write entertaining outdoor-life stories. In search of such a story, he and a *Times* photographer scooted across the entire steel girder length of the original Sunshine Skyway Bridge before it officially opened in 1954, claiming a "first to cross" title.

Allyn was also an inventor of sorts, or at least a wartime daydreamer. The likeable newspaperman claimed he spent most of his World War II navy submarine days on Midway Island dreaming about and designing the perfect outdoorsman watercraft. His vision was a flat-bottomed vessel with comfort features larger and more accommodating than those found on the "pig boats" on which he served. Top on his list was a satisfactory-size lavatory, or in mariner lingo, a head. Allyn wanted a vessel that was affordable, could be homebuilt and could be used to explore the waters of his beloved Florida "once this damn war was over."

As outdoors editor for the *Times*, he knew most, if not all, the boat designers and builders from Pensacola to Miami. Allyn showed his houseboat plans to anyone who would give him five minutes, and they all said he was crazy until one worn-down marine architect agreed to give "your Water Wagon a try." That established the brand name, and construction of the plywood craft started immediately.

The twenty-foot-long scow was an innovative combination of a camping trailer and self-trailering houseboat with a reinforced shallow-draw hull. The design allowed the vessel to navigate in open waters along the Florida coast and into some of its seldom-navigated rivers and streams. Powered by two small outboard motors, the Water Wagon could slide over obstacles such as fallen branches and even winch itself along to negotiate small sand bars or rock outcroppings.

Built with readily available materials and about a dozen sheets of plywood, Rube Allyn's boat was complete with a gas-stove galley, sleeping space for

Rube Allyn christened his first craft *Best Bet* after the title of his daily fishing advisory in the newspaper.

six, a stand-up shower and a landlubber-sized head. "After submarine duty I wanted a real toilet, with leg room, a magazine rack and a place to put your smokes and an ash tray," Allyn explained. "Not even a sub's captain had that luxury." Beds doubled as chairs for passenger comfort, and the cabin rooftop became a second deck where cots, chairs and a barbecue grill could be placed. Rube christened his first craft *Best Bet*, which was also the name of his regular fishing tip column.

Allyn preferred to write while on the go, doing something outdoors—experiencing the sun, the rain, the mosquitoes, the plants, birds and fish that abound in Florida—and then share that story rather than be confined to an office. Many of his articles for the *Times* were distributed nationally and generated considerable attention for St. Petersburg and the surrounding areas. "Fishing" and "paradise" were probably two of the most frequently used words in his tales that were believable, enticing and easily surpassed paid-for advertising in their value of attracting sportsmen to the Pinellas Peninsula.

One of his most notable efforts was a heavily illustrated *National Geographic* magazine story. On October 16, 1955, as he and his three-man crew made ready to depart, Vice-mayor Charles Kaniss instructed Allyn to carry

While a crowd of spectators looks on, Rube Allyn accepts the official flag of the St. Petersburg Yacht Club with instructions from Commander W.W. Jennings to fly it proudly as he "sails forth with good wishes from the city of St. Petersburg." *Courtesy of the* St. Petersburg Times.

greetings from St. Petersburg to all the cities and towns to be visited. The box-like houseboat proudly flew the St. Petersburg Yacht Club burgee in tandem with the official flag of the National Geographic Society.

The three-week voyage took the crew up the west coast with various excursions into rivers along the way, culminating with an eastward navigation of the state's best-known waterway, the Suwannee River. The following twenty-eight-page story with dozens of "Kodachromes by National Geographic Society photographer Bates Littlehales" was hugely popular with the magazine's international audience. That success prompted Allyn to publish the first of three books about Water Wagon voyages. Interestingly enough, he never patented the boat design and actually made the construction plans for the craft available free of charge through the outdoors department at the *St. Petersburg Times*.

Once again, word about St. Petersburg spread. The newspaper received more than 1,100 letters from around the country requesting the drawings. Allyn wrote in one daily column that literally hundreds of visitors had contacted him because he had whetted their appetite for Florida's outdoor recreation possibilities. St. Petersburg could chalk up yet another publicity point in its favor.

Allyn's *Dictionary of Fishes*, first published in 1952, sold so well it necessitated nine later editions and remains a classic authority on all species of Gulf of Mexico marine life. Later voyages southward and into the Everglades resulted in two additional printings of *Water Wagon: Through Florida Waterways by Scow and Outboard.*

Although Water Wagons were making waves in the boating world, locally, the Bee Line Ferry was about to sink into history. After nearly thirty years of operation, the ferry company was obsolete. Railways and waterways could no longer accommodate commuter demands. The *Tampa Tribune* lauded the two-lane Sunshine Skyway: "A mighty, massive yet graceful span of steel and stone, joint triumph of engineering and labor, it majestically reasserts the mastery of man the planner, man the builder" and graces the "sun kissed and Gulf-laved area of Florida's West Coast."

Barely missing a beat, St. Petersburg's chamber of commerce and local businesses highlighted the bridge in their promotions. The construction of the Skyway culminated decades of dreams to span Tampa Bay while ushering a new dawn for many more.

From George Gandy's "world's longest automobile toll-road," to the attention-commanding Sunshine Skyway Bridge, the Pinellas Peninsula no longer remained the remote hideaway that John Lodwick eagerly sold.

For decades, awe-struck tourists would continue to write letters home, extolling the virtues of Florida and its sun-filled beaches, but few would be published as they had been in years gone by.

There is little doubt that John Lodwick would have been humming the tune to the 1970s TV commercial proclaiming, "When you've got it bad, we've got it good." And the tourists would continue to come to the Florida shores, bringing their bulging wallets and "some-day" retirement dreams. For better or worse, St. Petersburg, the Sunshine City, could very well become "the City of Change."

EPILOGUE

Immediately following the death of John Lodwick, Nelson Poynter, president and editor of the *St. Petersburg Times*, wrote a glowing editorial of Lodwick's contributions and "the impetus his foresight and vision" had on the city. Through Lodwick's "vision and creative genius" in promoting St. Petersburg, he helped establish the Sunshine City as the "great winter capital of Florida's west coast," boasted the *Times* editor.

Nevertheless, Poynter also recognized that the days of ballyhoo and civic boosting had run their course. "With the fullest credit," Poynter wrote, "and appreciation of men like Mr. Lodwick who had the foresight to take advantage of them while they existed, it is improbable that such a combination of circumstances will ever again take place in Florida's history."

Who else besides John Lodwick would have the town's mayor parade through the streets of New York, wearing all white with a gaggle of beautiful, scantily clad women at his side, selling St. Petersburg or have that same mayor inspect bayside bathing suits on the "request" of the fictitious Purity League?

Only in Lodwick's St. Petersburg would shuffleboard, lawn bowling and checkers reach world championship status. And only the Sunshine City of his era could offer free newspapers when the sun failed to appear and make stars out of babies who never saw a cloudy day. "Perhaps," eulogized the *St. Petersburg Times*, "it is symbolic that the end of John Lodwick's career came at a time when the specialized era of development, in which he played so great a part, was in itself drawing to a close."

During his tenure working in promoting paradise, "John Lodwick's name was synonymous with St. Petersburg," touted city officials. However, the city of Lodwick's era was no more. For better or worse, the city of St. Petersburg had indeed transformed. The years of Depression had demonstrated St. Petersburg's need for diversification, and the war years forced civic officials to strive for growth and development outside the scope of the tourist trade.

Spurred by salacious advertising campaigns, subtropical winds and cheaper costs, well over 4 million tourists, armed with two weeks of vacation time and more disposable income than ever before, sought out Florida in 1950. The decade brought wave after wave of tourists to St. Petersburg, nearly half a million during the 1951–52 season alone.

In late 1954, as the Sunshine Skyway Bridge was connecting the final gap, St. Petersburg had blossomed into a "city full of promoters," suggested one report. "Some amateur and some ultra professional, but all of whom sing the praises of the Sunshine City." However, this influx perpetuated the city's aged public image.

Contradicting a 1960 newspaper release in the *New York Times*, which claimed the city's fifty thousand school-aged children to be proof positive that "St. Petersburg no longer considers itself an old folks' haven," the U.S. census continued recording increasing numbers of citizens over sixty-five years of age.

The 1950 figure of nearly 23 percent soared to an unprecedented high of 35 percent in 1970. When compared to a national average of about 11 percent, the long-standing national reputation and depreciatory view toward "God's Waiting Room" understandably remained.

Nevertheless, tourists came in droves. But the once famous green benches "suddenly disappeared," observed the *St. Petersburg Times*, "a none too subtle hint to the city's senior citizens that their welcome was not so durable after all."

By 1970, the annual tally of vehicles crossing the Sunshine Skyway topped 3 million, prompting the addition of an identical sister span to shuttle tourists to and from St. Petersburg. Florida turnstiles would soon spin uncontrollably at Walt Disney's 1971 grand gala in Orlando; a record 1.7 million tourists would visit Disney World that year.

Shaking off the effects of the mid-1980s national energy crisis, the tourist trade would pour nearly $2 billion into the local economy. On the eve of the twenty-first century, the same area had spent more than $3 million in advertising yet recorded an amazing 11 million day and overnight visitors.

Prior to 1950, barely a dozen states actively promoted tourism. By 1980, every state in the Union had become active in tourism development. The availability of DDT and air-conditioning would eventually make Florida a prime destination choice. As Florida's number one industry—creating nearly 20 percent of the state's total economy—tourism generated $51.5 billion and drew in some 74.5 million tourists to the Sunshine State in 2003.

Regardless of the product or service offered, advertising is not just a step-by-step discipline. It comes in many forms that change with the times and technology. John Lodwick had his postcards and practically unlimited access to northern newspaper society columns. Today, we have the Internet and an almost endless supply of advertising venues from sporting events to celebrity endorsements.

And it would appear that the city of St. Petersburg is no exception to the favored rule of ad agency folk who have long advised clients that "if business is bad, you have to advertise; but if business is good, you must advertise."

In October 2008, the *St. Petersburg Times* reported a decline in downtown business activity, noting that "as the economy continues to spiral down, downtown's claim as Tampa Bay's hottest neighborhood is becoming increasingly vulnerable."

However, *Times* staffer Cristina Silva also quoted Mayor Rick Baker, who echoed the views of his predecessors, "I still think St. Petersburg, right now on the west coast of Florida, is considered the place to be."

The article noted that some business owners complain the city isn't doing enough to attract people to the area and has a "paltry marketing budget." Some critics, Silva reported, argue that while Tampa spent nearly $150,000 just to promote Ybor City, St. Petersburg spent only $75,000 on advertising for the entire year.

Nevertheless, John Lodwick—the early architect of "world class" and "championship" events—would probably applaud Mayor Baker's efforts at securing local events like the Grand Prix, Miss Florida Pageant and the St. Petersburg Bowl. And one can only imagine how John Lodwick and Al Lang would be firing off press releases and exchanging high-fives over the possibility of St. Petersburg hosting the 2008 American League Championship Series with their own Tampa Bay Rays hot on the trail to a World Series.

In early September 2013, an NBC *Today Show* segment, videotaped in St. Petersburg and hosted by veteran broadcaster Jane Pauley, aired nationally and was also posted on the World Wide Web.

Produced as part of her "Life Reimagined" series of stories, Pauley introduced viewers to St. Petersburg resident Rich Luker, "sixty years old and going on eleven," and talked about the newfound satisfaction he discovered

when he joined the Half Century Softball Club that plays at the city's North Shore Ballpark. That ball diamond isn't Florida's fabled Fountain of Youth, but for Luker and his age fifty-plus teammates, it comes close.

Baseball, health and sunshine!

The promotion of paradise today may be more subtle and polished, but without a doubt, the message still resonates. And for St. Petersburg, Florida, there's still plenty of sunshine to sell.

SELECTED BIBLIOGRAPHY

Books

Akin, Edward N. *Flagler: Rockefeller Partner and Florida Baron.* Kent, OH: Kent State University Press, 1988.

Allyn, Rube. *Water Wagon: Through Florida Waterways by Scow and Outboard.* New York: Farrar, Straus & Giroux, 1952

Andersen, Hans Christian, and Mike Robinson. *Literature and Tourism: Essays in the Reading and Writing of Tourism.* London: Thomson Learning, 2003.

Arsenault, Raymond O. *St. Petersburg and the Florida Dream, 1880–1950.* Norfolk, VA: Donning Co., 1988.

Ayers, R. Wayne. *St. Petersburg: The Sunshine City.* Charleston, SC: Arcadia Publishing, 2001.

Barbour, George. *Florida for Tourists, Invalids, and Settlers.* New York: D. Appleton and Company, 1884.

Beecher, Eunice White. "Mrs. Henry Ward Beecher." *Letters from Florida.* New York: D. Appleton and Company, 1879.

Bill, Ledyard. *A Winter in Florida.* New York: Wood & Holdbrook, 1869.

Bivans, Ann-Marie. *Miss America: In Pursuit of the Crown.* New York: Mastermedia Ltd., 1991.

Burnett, Gene. *Florida's Past.* Vol. 2. Sarasota, FL: Pineapple Press, 1988.

Coppersmith, Jonathan. *From Lemons to Lemonade: The Development of AP Wirephoto.* College Station: Texas A&M University, 2000.

Douglas, Marjory S. *Florida: The Long Frontier.* New York: Harper & Row, 1967.

Dunn, Hampton. *Yesterday's St. Petersburg.* Miami, FL: E.A. Seemann Pub., 1973.

Federal Court Reporter. *Cases Argued and Determined in the Circuit Courts of Appeals and District Courts of the United States.* Vol. 253. St. Paul, MN: West Publishing Co., December 1919.

Federal Writers Project. *Florida: A Guide to the Southernmost State.* New York: Oxford University Press, 1939.

Feifer, Maxine. *Tourism in History*. New York: Stein and Day, 1985.

Frazer, William, and John Guthrie Jr. *The Florida Land Boom: Speculation, Money and the Banks*. Westport, CT: Quorum Books, 1995.

Fuller, Walter P. *St. Petersburg and Its People.* St. Petersburg, FL: Great Outdoors Publishing, 1972.

———. *This Was Florida's Boom*. St. Petersburg, FL: Times Pub. Co., 1954.

Gannon, Michael. *Florida, a Short History*. Gainesville: University Press of Florida, 2003.

Garner, Gretchen. *Disappearing Witness, Change in Twentieth Century American Photography*. Baltimore, MD: Johns Hopkins University Press, 2003.

Gordon Patterson, "The Creation of the Florida Anti-Mosquito Association." In *Paradise Lost?: The Environmental History of Florida*. Edited by Jack E. Davis and Raymond Arsenault. Gainesville: University Press of Florida, 2005: 165–73.

Grismer, Karl. *The Story of St. Petersburg: The History of Lower Pinellas Peninsula and the Sunshine City*. St. Petersburg, FL: P.K Smith and Co., 1948.

Henshall, James A. *Camping and Cruising in Florida: An Account of Two Winters Passed in Cruising Around the Coasts of Florida as Viewed from the Standpoint of an Angler, a Sportsman, a Yachtsman, a Naturalist, and a Physician*. Cincinnati, OH: R. Clarke & Co., 1884.

Holden, Andrew. *Environment and Tourism.* New York: Routledge, 2000.

Hurley, Frank T., Jr. *Surf, Sand and Postcard Sunsets: A History of Pass-A-Grille and the Gulf Beaches*. St. Petersburg, FL: Great Outdoors Pub., 1977.

Jackson, Kenneth T. "The Crabgrass Frontier: 150 Years of Suburban Growth in America." In *The Urban Experience: Themes in American History*. Edited by Raymond A. Mohl and James F. Richardson. Belmont, CA: Wadsworth Pub. Co., 1973: 211–7.

Jackson, Page S. *St. Petersburg: An Informal History*. St. Petersburg, FL: Great Outdoors Publishing Co., 1962.

Kline, Gary T. *The Official N.H.P.A. History of the World Tournament, 1909–1980*. Dayton, OH: Reflection Press, 1922.

Monmonier, Mark. *Air Apparent*. Chicago: University of Chicago Press, 2000.

Mormino, Gary. *Land of Sunshine, State of Dreams: A Social History of Modern Florida*. Gainesville: University Press of Florida, 2005.

———. "World War II." In *The New History of Florida*. Edited by Michael Gannon. Gainesville: University Press of Florida, 1996.

Ogilvie, F.W. *The Tourist Movement: An Economic Study*. London: P.S. King and Sons, 1933.

Orrick, Bentley, and Harry L. Crumpacker. *The Tampa Tribune: A Century of Florida Journalism.* Tampa, FL: University of Tampa Press, 1998.

Pederson, Paul. *Build It and They Will Come: The Arrival of the Tampa Bay Devil Rays*. Stuart: Florida Sports Press, 1997.

Roberts, Kenneth L. *Sun Hunting: Adventures and Observations Among the Native and Migratory Tribes of Florida, Including the Stoical Time-Killers of Palm Beach, the Gentle and Gregarious Tin-Canners of the Remote Interior, and the Vivacious and Semi-Violent Peoples of Miami and Its Purlieus.* Indianapolis, IN: Bobbs-Merrill, 1922.

Stephenson, R. Bruce. *Visions of Eden: Environmentalism, Urban Planning, and City Building in St. Petersburg, Florida, 1900–1995.* Columbus: Ohio University Press, 1997.

Stewart, J.D., ed. *The History of the Bench and Bar of Missouri.* N.p.: The Legal Publishing Co, 1898: 611.

Stockbridge, Frank P., and John H. Perry. *Florida in the Making.* New York: De Bower Pub. Co., 1926.

———. *So This Is Florida.* Jacksonville, FL: John H. Perry Pub. Co., 1938.

Susman, Warren. "Cultural Heroes: Ford, Barton, Ruth." In *Culture as History: The Transformation of American Society in the Twentieth Century*. Edited by Warren I. Susman. New York: Pantheon, 1984: 122–49.

Tyler, Daniel F. *Where to Go in Florida.* New York: Hopcraft, 1881.

Waitley, Douglas. *Roadside History of Florida.* Missoula, MT: Mountain Press Pub. Co., 1997.

Wynne, Nick. *Tin Can Tourists in Florida, 1900–1970.* Charleston, SC: Arcadia Press, 1999.

Young, June. *St. Petersburg: An Oral History*. Charleston, SC: Arcadia Publications, 2002.

Zimmerman, William. *William Wrigley, Jr., The Man and His Business, 1861–1932.* N.p.: R.R. Donnelley & Sons Company, at the Lakeside Press, 1935.

Newspapers and Periodicals

Allyn, Rube. "Cruising Florida's Western Waterways." *National Geographic Society Magazine* 108 (January 1955): 49–76.

———. "Cruising Florida's Western Waterways." *National Geographic Magazine* 107, no. 1 (January 1955).

Arsenault, Raymond. "A Blimp Went Up and the Market Crashed." *St. Petersburg Times,* June 8, 1988.

Atkins, Holly. "Wonders of Florida." *St. Petersburg Times,* May 27, 2002.

Bothwell, Dick. "79 Today, Ex-Mayor Pulver Has Career Like Horatio Alger Novel." *St. Petersburg Times,* November 12, 1949.

Brooklyn Eagle. "The Mecca of Health Seekers." April 17, 1898.

"Chamber of Commerce Bulletin for April, 1924." St. Petersburg Museum of History Archives: Chamber of Commerce Collection.

"Chamber of Commerce Bulletin for May, 1924." St. Petersburg Museum of History Archives: Chamber of Commerce Collection.

"Charm School." *Collier's Magazine* (January 16, 1947): cover, 17.

Chicago Daily Tribune. "St. Petersburg's Advertising and Tourist Tardy." December 24, 1935.

Crane, Jeanette. "We Will Be Known by What We Preserve." *St. Petersburg Evening Independent*, May 25, 1979.

Danville Bee. "Establish Southern Base for Baby Blimp." November 27, 1928.

———. "Wives Ask Mayor to Shield Hubbies from Sea Vamps." February 17, 1922.

Evening Independent. "Greyhound Turns Movie Star for Television." December 29, 1949: 13.

———. "Kenmuir to Leave Sept 7th on Tenth Good Will Tour." August 1, 1945: front page.

———. "Local Printers Get City Work." August 9, 1927, 1.
———. "Major Brown Founds City's Fame." September 1, 1950.
———. "Miami Might Be in Market for Sunshine Pullman, Governors Told." August 30, 1927, 5.
———. "Motor Club Official Sees Evidence of Heavier Travel to Florida." August 9, 1927, 1.
———. "Publicity Given Sunshine Pullman in Northern Press," October 14, 1926, 7.
———. "Smith Filmed City For TV." September 26, 1969, 20.
———. "William Kenmuir Rites Set for Next Monday; His Death Called Loss to City by Host of Friends." December 15, 1944, 1.
Florida Times-Union. "St. Petersburg Claims State Tourist Crown." May 7, 1946.
Fort Wayne Journal Gazette. "Wives Ask Mayor to Shield Their Husbands from Wiles of Sea Vamps." February 9, 1922.
Graham, Jane. "City Publicity Bureau Had Its Inception in Blizzard in the North." *Evening Independent*, November 7, 1938.
Hammond Times. "All Sunshine No Clouds in their Young Lives!" November 15, 1935.
Hartzell, Scott T. "Mayor Thrived on Stunts, Infighting." *St. Petersburg Times*, November 2, 1999.
Heard, J.W. "St. Petersburg, Fla., The Ideal City by the Sea." *St. Petersburg Times*, September 1899.
Huntley, Helen. "The Story Behind the Old Painting." *St. Petersburg Times*, January 17, 1971.
Jones, Malcolm. "A City Built on Changing Dreams." *St. Petersburg Times*, February 12, 1989.
Lodwick, John. "Boating Events Enliven Days at St. Petersburg." *Chicago Daily Tribune*, February 1, 1931.
———. "Charlestonians Are Attracted by Charity Events at St. Petersburg." *Charleston Gazette*, December 27, 1931.
———. "Gala Season Opens at Florida Resort." *Hammond Times*, January 16, 1938.
———. "Kingstonians at St. Petersburg." *Kingston Daily Freeman*, February 26, 1931.
———. "Local Tourist at St. Petersburg." *Indiana Evening Gazette*, January 9, 1932.
———. "Olean People Vacation in Sunny South." *Olean Herald*, May 16, 1931.
———. "Puritan to make Flight to Florida." *Key West Citizen*, November 7, 1928.
———. "Quoits and Horseshoes Easy for all Juniors." *Oakland Tribune*, April 29, 1926.
———. "Southland's First Airship Base Located at St. Petersburg." *Cedar Rapids Tribune*, December 28, 1928.
———. "St. Petersburg Awaiting Half Million Guests." *Chicago Daily Tribune*, December 11, 1938.
———. "St. Petersburg Has a Tonic for Nation's Nerves." *Chicago Daily Tribune*, December 7, 1941.
———. "St. Petersburg Sun Bathing Season On as Northland Shivers from Cold." *Circleville Herald*, February 9, 1929.
———. "The Voice of the Traveler." *Chicago Daily Tribune*, January 18, 1942.
Mansfield News-Journal. "All Sunshine, No Clouds in Their Young Lives." December 13, 1935.

McClure, Rhyder. "The Men Who Bridged the Bay." *St. Petersburg Times*, July 14, 1980.

Monk, Jean. "St. Petersburg Is Playground, Reporter Finds." *St. Petersburg Times*, January 11, 1936.

Morgan, Philip. "Sunshine Skyway's History Spans 45 Years." *Tampa Tribune*, September 6, 1999.

Mullins, Miriam. "The Day the War Ended: A Remembrance." *St. Petersburg Times*, July 25, 1995.

New Mexican. "104 Lovely Leg—But Not Shoddy Show." September 3, 1963.

New York Times. "Asks Bathing Suit Censor." January 26, 1922.

———. February 1, 1942.

———. "Florida Tourists Are Spending Less." January 29, 1933.

———. "Fortunate Fifties—St. Petersburg Counts Its Blessing, Cites Rapid Growth in Decade." November 6, 1960.

———. "Gulf Towns Busy Building Bedrooms." December 14, 1952.

———. "Happy Days Are Here Again." January 7, 1934.

———. "Here Is Your Place in the Sun." December 2, 1934.

———. "I'll See You in Sunny St. Petersburg." December 10, 1933.

———. January 18, 1942.

———. January 1, 1933.

———. January 7, 1923.

———. January 21, 1923.

———. "John Lodwick." October 17, 1942.

———. October 4, 1942.

———. "Wonderful Winter Playground Between the Gulf and Tampa Bay." December 13, 1925.

Oklahoma Ada Evening News. "Miss America Pageant Turns into a Refined-Type Lady." September 1, 1963.

Oliver, Wayne. "Al Lang Is Known as Ambassador of Baseball Clubs." *Ogden Standard-Examiner*, April 1, 1942.

Racine Journal News. "Help! Sea Vamps Capture St. Pete's Bachelor Mayor." March 7, 1922.

Reno Evening Gazette. "Bathing Suit Inspector Requested in Florida." January 25, 1922.

Richter, Linda K. "State-Sponsored Tourism." *Public Administration Review* 45, no. 6. (November–December 1985): 832–9.

Rivers, William. "City Full of Promoters." *Panama City News Herald*, August 22, 1954.

Rogers, David K. "Proposal to Honor Editor Is Under Fire." *St. Petersburg Times*, November 25, 1997.

Schnur, Jim. "In Search of 'Health City,' but finding Yellow Fever." *Punta Pinal Newsletter* (Pinellas County Historical Society) 32, no. 2 (June 2005).

Snell, C. Perry. "Hours of Toil Bring Success to Enterprise." *St. Petersburg Times*, January 30, 1927.

St. Petersburg Times. "Braves Pound Five Indian Hurlers for 11–5 Victory." October 11, 1948: 10.

———. "C. of C. Plans Drive to Bring War Workers Here." June 29, 1943.

———. "Campaign Launched to Get $20,000 Fund to Advertise the City." December 19, 1918.
———. "City Now Large Enough to Have Both Tourists and Industries." December 24, 1941.
———. "City Park System Owes Its Growth to Snell's Help." January 30, 1927.
———. "City Planning Page Ad in Post; Also to Use Smaller Space." July 30, 1924, 3.
———. "City Plans Ads in 44 Papers, 12 Magazines." September 9, 1943.
———. "Famous Sunshine Pullman Sold to City of Miami for $5,000." March 31, 1928, 11.
———. "$50,000 Ad Fund for City Urged." June 22, 1943.
———. "Former Sunshine Pullman May Be Barred from Tour." April 3, 1929: 6.
———. "Great Throng Bids Welcome to Governors" November 21, 1924.
———. "Helped Build Better City, Mayor States." October 17, 1942.
———. "John Lodwick Dies Suddenly." October 17, 1942.
———. "John Lodwick—End of an Era." October 17, 1942.
———. "Papers Tell of White Way." July 30, 1924, 10.
———. "St. Petersburg and Tampa United." November 20, 1924, 1A.
———. "Scotch Band Want Pelican, Stuffed One Would Be Added to Exhibit in Sunshine Pullman." April 30, 1925, 2.
———. "Solarium Society Members Aren't Interested in Nudism Movement, President Explains." March 5, 1936, 2.1.
———. "Water Wagon Brings Visitors." October 13, 1952.
Straub, William L. Editorial. *St. Petersburg Times*, November 6, 1932.
Tampa Daily Times. "Florida Urged to Seek Fame as Health Center." April 12, 1933.
———. "Sunshine City Is Advertising." March 15, 1919.
Tampa Tribune. "Tourism Officials to Spend an Extra $750,000 to Attract Visitors." November 8, 1995.
"Tourism: A Good Value for Pinellas County." *Suncoast Magazine* (October 1985).
Vidette-Messenger. "Florida City Film Shown to Rotary." February 22, 1944.
Wall Street Journal. "Eastern Air Transport." December 19, 1930.
———. "Florida Construction." January 9, 1926.
———. "Florida Migration Heavy." January 7, 1935.
———. "Florida Travel Heavy." January 12, 1933.
———. "Gandy Bridge." January 14, 1926.
———. "More Florida Tourists." May 20, 1933.
Warner, Richard. "Florida Gulf Shores–West Coast Communities Report Record Season with Crowds Still Arriving." *New York Times*, March 2, 1952.
Weiss, Thomas. "Tourism in America Before World War II." *Journal of Economic History* 64, no. 2 (2004): 289–327.

Interviews

Hurley, Frank, Jr. Interview with author, June 17, 2006.
Mogavero, Jari. Interview with author. Gulf Beaches Museum of History, St. Pete Beach, FL, April 1, 2006.

Shewmaker, Jackie. Interview with author. Gulf Beaches Museum of History. St. Pete Beach, FL, March 25, 2006.

Swenningsen, Jack. Interview with author, March 3, 2012; August 4, 2013; September 2, 2013.

Other

Culp, Susan O'Brien. "For the Duration: Women's Roles in St. Petersburg and Tampa During World War II." *Tampa Bay History* 17 (Spring/Summer 1995): 16–33.

Davis, F.A. *Facts and Suggestions for Persons Forced to Seek Permanent or Temporary Homes on the Pinellas Peninsula*. Philadelphia, PA: F.A. Davis Pub. Co., 1896.

———. *Progress and Possibilities of St. Petersburg*. Philadelphia, PA: F.A. Davis Pub. Co., 1901.

———. *Souvenir—St. Petersburg, the Pleasure City of the South*. Philadelphia, PA: F.A. Davis Pub. Co., 1906.

Dunn, Hampton. "Ponce De Leon Slept Here: A History of Tourism in Florida." Hampton Dunn Collection, Special Collections, University of South Florida.

ERA Druggists' Directory. 17th Edition. New York: D.O. Haynes & CO., 1913–14.

Florida and Southern Winter Resorts. Promotional pamphlet. United States Railroad Administration, 1919.

"Florida Health Notes." *Florida Board of Health*, February 1914.

Florida: Souvenir of Florida Convention of Investment Bankers at St. Petersburg, December 6 to 12, 1925. St. Petersburg Museum of History, Chamber of Commerce Collection.

"Florida: The Playground of the Nation." *Florida Gazetteer*. R.L. Polk and Co., 1925.

"From Sidelines to the Field." Life Reimagined. http://lifereimagined.aarp.org/janepauley/3701-From-the-Sidelines-to-the-Field (accessed September 15, 2013).

Mormino, Gary. *Hillsborough Goes to War: The Home Front, 1940–1950,* Tampa, FL: Tampa Bay History Center, 2001.

Pinellas Planning Council. Historical Background of Pinellas County, FL.

Pulver, Frank "My Announcement for Mayor." *Campaign Flyer*. St. Petersburg, FL: Tourist Press, 1921.

Roosevelt, Franklin D. *Joint Address to Congress Requesting a Declaration of War*. December 8, 1941. Records of the U.S. Senate. SEN 77A-H1. Record Group 46. National Archives. Washington, D.C.

St. Petersburg Board of Trade. Promotional pamphlet, circa 1919. St. Petersburg Museum of History, Chamber of Commerce Collections.

St. Petersburg Chamber of Commerce promotional films, circa 1944–50. St. Petersburg Museum of History, Video Archive Collection.

U.S. Patent Office. Pulver US625803 A. Google U.S. Patent Office Search. https://www.google.com/patents/US625803?dq=frank+pulver&hl=en&sa=X&ei=faQoUuroBKS8sASd_YHgBQ&ved=0CDUQ6wEwAA (accessed April 12, 2013).

U.S. Railroad Administration. *Florida and Southern Winter Resorts*. 1919.

Van Bibber, Washington Chew. "Peninsular and Sub-Peninsular Air and Climates: A Contribution to Sanitary Science, Relating Especially to the Climate and Healthfulness of Pinellas Peninsula, Florida." 1885.

INDEX

ABOUT THE AUTHOR

Nevin D. Sitler is the director of education and outreach at the St. Petersburg Museum of History and holds a master's degree in Florida studies from the University of South Florida–St. Petersburg. In 2013, he coauthored *The Sunshine Skyway Bridge: Spanning Tampa Bay*, also published by The History Press. He is a contributing author for *Florida's Historic Places* (2012) and *The Rivers of the Green Swamp Anthology* (2008) and provided historical consultation for *Florida's Fabulous Lighthouses* (2007) and *Florida: Celebrate the States* (2006). Nevin has written various magazine and newspaper articles, including the popular "St. Pete's Past" weekly feature in the *St. Petersburg Times* (*Tampa Bay Times*). He is a contributor to several historical and Florida-themed websites and regularly assists professional writers and student researchers.